GW01150178

Lance Salway's book of **Gold and Gold-Hunters**

GOOD NEWS
FOR
MINERS.

NEW GOODS,
PROVISIONS, TOOLS,
CLOTHING, &c. &c.

GREAT BARGAINS!
JUST RECEIVED BY THE SUBSCRIBERS, AT THE LARGE TENT ON THE HILL,

A superior Lot of New, Valuable and most DESIRABLE GOODS for Miners and for residents also. Among them are the following:

STAPLE PROVISIONS AND STORES.

Pork, Flour, Bread, Beef, Hams, Mackerel, Sugar, Molasses, Coffee, Teas, Butter & Cheese, Pickles, Beans, Peas, Rice, Chocolate, Spices, Salt, Soap, Vinegar, &c.

EXTRA PROVISIONS AND STORES.

Every variety of Preserved Meats and Vegetables and Fruits, [more than eighty different kinds.] Tongues and Sounds; Smoked Halibut; Dry Cod Fish; Eggs fresh and fine; Figs, Raisins, Almonds and Nuts; China Preserves; China Bread and Cakes; Butter Crackers, Boston Crackers, and many other very desirable and *choice bits*.

DESIRABLE GOODS FOR COMFORT AND HEALTH.

Patent Cot Bedsteads, Mattresses and Pillows, Blankets and Comforters. Also, in Clothing—Overcoats, Jackets, Miner's heavy Velvet Coats and Pantaloons, Woolen Pants, Guernsey Frocks, Flannel Shirts and Drawers, Stockings and Socks, Boots, Shoes; Rubber Waders, Coats, Blankets, &c.

MINING TOOLS, &c.; BUILDING MATERIALS, &c.

Cradles, Shovels, Spades, Hoes, Picks, Axes, Hatchets, Hammers; every variety of Workman's Tools, Nails, Screws, Brads, &c.

SUPERIOR GOLD SCALES.   MEDICINE CHESTS, &c.

Superior Medicine Chests, well assorted, together with the principal Important Medicines for Dysentery, Fever and Fever and Ague, Scurvy, &c.

N.B.–Important Express Arrangement for Miners.

The Subscribers will run an EXPRESS to and from every Steamer, carrying and returning Letters for the Post Office and Expresses to the States. Also, conveying "*GOLD DUST*" or Parcels, to and from the Mines to the Banking Houses, or the several Expresses for the States, insuring their safety.——The various NEWSPAPERS, from the Eastern, Western and Southern States, will also be found on sale at our stores, together with a large stock of *BOOKS* and *PAMPHLETS* constantly on hand.

Excelsior Tent, Mormon Island,
    January 1, 1850.

ALTA CALIFORNIA PRESS.

WARREN & CO.

Lance Salway's book of
Gold and Gold-Hunters

Illustrated by Chris Molan
and with prints and photographs

KESTREL BOOKS

FOR JOHN AND EVELYN EVANS

KESTREL BOOKS
Published by Penguin Books Ltd
Harmondsworth, Middlesex, England

This anthology copyright © 1978 by Lance Salway
Illustrations Copyright © 1978 by Chris Molan
The acknowledgements on page 7 constitute an extension of this copyright page.

All rights reserved. No part of this publication may be reproduced, stored in a retrieval system, or transmitted in any form or by any means, electronic, mechanical, photocopying, recording, or otherwise, without the prior permission of the Copyright owner.

First published in 1978 by Kestrel Books

ISBN 0 7226 5419 7

Printed in Great Britain by
Butler & Tanner Ltd
Frome and London

Contents

Acknowledgements 7

1 The lure of gold 11

2 Gold of the gods 16
   The child of Zeus 16
   Ants, griffins and one-eyed men 18

3 The gold makers 23
   A noble medicine 24
   The mysterious visitor 26

4 Gold of the New World 31
   Gold is most excellent 31
   The tears of the sun 35
   The search for El Dorado 44

5 The great gold rushes 45
   'Some kind of mettle that looks like goald' 45
   The California Trail 47
   Rocking the cradle 54
   All that glitters ... 59
   Gold down under 67
   Off to the Klondike! 72
   The Dead Horse Trail 78
   St Patrick's Day at All Gold Creek 82

6 Gold robbers – and smugglers 87
   How Hangtown got its name 87
   Black Bart 89
   The ordeal of Ellen Clacy 92
   A remarkable and daring outrage 96
   The great bullion robbery 99
   Gold in the sky 102

7 Hidden gold 108
   The tomb of Tutankhamen 109
   The treasure of the Incas 114
   The wreck of the Laurentic 118
   'All the gold in Germany' 121
   Lasseter's reef 123
   The curse of the Lost Dutchman 126

8 The hunt goes on 129
   Two miles down 129
   Gold on your doorstep 132

Index 135

Acknowledgements

The author and publishers would like to thank the following for their kind permission to reproduce illustrative material: Associated Press for pp. 122 and 123 *both*; Australian Information Service, London, for pp. 11 and 71 *below*; the Bancroft Library for p. 2; B. T. Batsford for p. 21; the Trustees of the British Museum for pp. 12 *above right* and *below*, 13 *left both* and *above right*, 19 and 39; Camera Press for pp. 103 (Photo: Adrian Flowers) and 108; Canadian Public Archives for pp. 74, 75 and 79; *Century Magazine* (November 1890 to April 1891, Volume XLI) for p. 45; Chamber of Mines of South Africa for p. 130; Dumbarton Oaks, Washington DC for p. 43 *below left*; EMI Limited for p. 14; Griffith Institute, Ashmolean Museum, for pp. 12 *above left*, 110, 111 and 113; Gwynedd Archive Service for p. 133 *above right* and *below*; Robert Harding Associates for pp. 40 and 43 *above both* and *below right*; E. J. Holmyard, *Alchemy* (Penguin, 1968) for pp. 23 and 25; Mark Howell and Tony Morrison, *Steps To A Fortune* (Geoffrey Bles, 1967) for p. 115; the Huntingdon Library, San Marino, California for pp. 52 *both*, 53 *below*, 60 and 66 (HM 8044, Numbers 11, 51, 123); Keystone Press for pp. 104 *both* and 105 *both*; Kunsthistorische Museum, Vienna for p. 13 *below*; Mansell Collection for pp. 46 *below*, 47, 70 *below*, 71 *above*, 73 and 131 *below*; Mary Evans Picture Library for pp. 62 and 68; National Library of Australia for pp. 70 *above* (Rex Nan Kivell Collection 703), 93 (Watercolour by G. Lacey) and 97 (Engraving by McFarlane and Erskine from David Blair, *History of Australasia*, 1879); National Museum of Wales for p. 133 *above left*; Glen Chesney Quiett, *Pay Dirt, A Panorama of American Gold Rushes* (D. Appleton-Century Company, 1936) for pp. 65 (engraving by Nordhoff, California, 1872) and 89; Radio Times Hulton Picture Library for pp. 30 and 61; Royal Canadian Mounted Police for p. 81; South Africa House for pp. 129 and 131 *above*; Wells Fargo Bank History Room for p. 59 *below*; Western Americana Picture Library for pp. 34, 46 *above*, 50, 53 *above*, 57 and 59 *above*.

The publishers and author would like to thank the following for their kind permission to reproduce extracts from copyright material: Angus & Robertson Publishers, Sydney: *Lasseter's Last Ride*, copyright © Ion L. Idriess, 1931 (pp. 124–5); Geoffrey Bles, London: *Steps to a Fortune: Adventure in the Andes* by Mark Howell and Tony Morrison, 1967 (pp. 115–18); Cambridge University Press: 'Notes on the "Laurentic" Salvage Operations and the Prevention of Compressed Air Illness' by G. C. C. Damant in *Journal of Hygiene*, vol. XXV, no. 1, February 1926 (pp. 119–21); Curtis Brown Academic: *The Tomb of Tutankhamen*, vol. I, by Howard Carter and A. C. Mace, 1923 (pp. 109–14); Columbia University Press, New York: *Gold Rush: The Journals, Drawings and Other Papers of J. Goldsborough Bruff*, edited by G. W. Read and R. Gaines, 1949 (pp. 50–54); John Farquharson Ltd: *The Killer Mountains: A Search for the Legendary Lost Dutchman Mine* by Curt Gentry, 1971 (pp. 126–8); Robert Hale: *Lust for Gold* by Garry Hogg, 1960 (pp. 24–6, 90–92, 121–3); Harvard University Press/William Heinemann: *Diodorus Siculus, Diodorus of Sicily*, translated by C. H. Oldfather (The Loeb Classical Library), 1935 (pp. 20–22); Michael Joseph: *The Smugglers: An Investigation into the World of the Contemporary Smuggler* by Timothy Green, 1969 (pp. 106–7); Penguin Books: *The Metamorphoses of Ovid*, translated by Mary M. Innes, 1955 (p. 17), *Herodotus: The Histories*, translated by Aubrey de Selincourt, 1972 (pp. 18–20, 27–9), *Alchemy* by E. J. Holmyard, 1957 (pp. 27–9) and *The Four Voyages of Christopher Columbus*, edited and translated by J. M. Cohen, 1969 (pp. 31–5); Ridge Press Inc., New York: *House of Bondage* by Ernest Cole with Thomas Flaherty, 1968 (pp. 130–32); Routledge & Kegan Paul Ltd: *The Hard Road to Klondike* by Michael MacGowan, translated from the Irish by Valentin Iremonger, 1962 (pp. 82–6).

Whilst every effort has been made to trace copyright holders of material included in this book, the publishers apologize if any material has inadvertently been included without permission having been obtained.

THE ROUTES TO THE KLONDIKE

ALASKA
CANADA
Norton Sound
Yukon River
Fort Yukon
St Michael
THE RICH MAN'S ROUTE
Mackenzie River
Dawson City
Klondike River
Stewart River
USA
Valdez
Pelly River
White Pass (The Dead Horse Trail)
Chilkoot Pass
Yukon River
Dyea
Skagway
BRITISH COLUMBIA
Kilometres 800

THE CALIFORNIA TRAIL

OREGON
IDAHO
Sacramento River
Sutter's Fort
Snake River
Fort Hall
WYOMING
South Pass
Humboldt River
Great Salt Lake
N. Platte River
Fort
San Francisco
Sink
Salt Lake City
Fort Bridger
NEVADA
UTAH
S. Platte River
CALIFORNIA
COLORADO
Kilometres 800

Klondike

N. AMERICA

San Francisco
THE CALIFORNIA TRAIL
Independence
New York

THE MAIN ROUTES TO CALIFORNIA

Panama

PACIFIC OCEAN

S. AMERICA

ATLANTIC OCEAN

Key

● Gold Deposits

→ Gold Routes

ASIA

MISSOURI

Kearny
Independence

INDIA

PACIFIC OCEAN

INDIAN OCEAN

AUSTRALIA

1. The lure of gold

The story of man's search for gold is as long as recorded time. No other metal has so captivated the human mind, and no other natural substance has been the cause of so much bloodshed and violence. Men and women have travelled across the world to seek it, proud nations have been destroyed by it, men have killed and been killed in their efforts to obtain it. It is an exciting story but a violent one, a story that will not end until all the gold in the world has been found and exploited.

But what *is* gold, and why is it the most coveted of metals? A geological definition of gold would be that it is a yellow, malleable and ductile metallic element that occurs naturally in the uncombined state. This brief description holds all the factors which have influenced man's desire to possess it.

In the beginning, its appeal was aesthetic and mystical: the shining yellow beauty of gold came to symbolize the majesty of the gods, and its permanence reflected their immortality. The ease with which the metal could be worked resulted in its use as decoration, and its rarity soon ensured its value as evidence of wealth. Gold became a symbol of power and riches, and kings and commoners alike yearned to possess it.

The durability of gold has always been its

Above: *the Welcome nugget, one of the largest pieces of gold yet found. It weighed 2217 oz 16 dwt and was 99·2 per cent pure gold. It was found at Bakery Hill, Victoria, on 10 June 1858*

Top left: *profile from Tutankhamen's funeral mask*

Top right: *gold open-work dagger handle from China, fourth century* BC

Left: *late-bronze-age gold collar from Cintra, near Lisbon, Portugal*

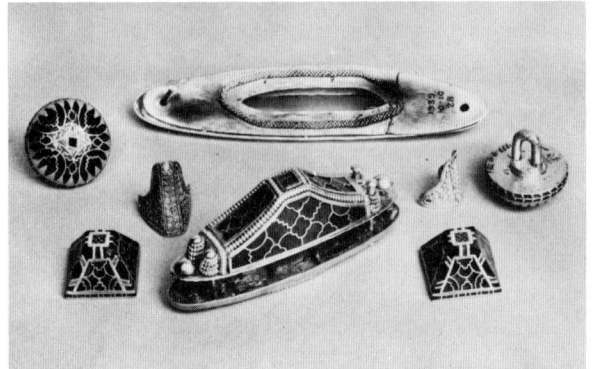

Top left: *a gold clasp from the Sutton Hoo ship burial*

Above: *more Anglo-Saxon treasure from the Sutton Hoo ship burial: the fittings of a sword in gold with garnets and coloured glass*

Top right: *a gold buckle from the Sutton Hoo ship burial. It dates from the seventh century AD*

Right: *the magnificent Cellini salt cellar made for François I of France, and now in the Kunsthistorisches Museum, Vienna*

Gold and Gold-Hunters

Nowadays if you sell over a million records you will probably be awarded a golden disc (though it usually contains only 0·03 grams of real gold). André Previn received his for selling over a million copies of his classical recordings

greatest strength. Unlike other metals it does not tarnish. It does not corrode or rust or flake, and the only chemical which can affect it is a mixture of nitric and hydrochloric acid. The golden treasures of Tutankhamen are as dazzling today as they were when his tomb was sealed thousands of years ago, and gold coins raised from sunken Spanish galleons gleam as brightly now as they did when the waves closed over them. Gold fillings in teeth resist decay, and the durability of a gold wedding ring is equated with the permanence of the marriage vows. It is hardly surprising, then, that gold should come to be linked with immortality, or that the medieval alchemists should devote their energies to the search for a substance which would not only transform base metals into gold but which would also grant everlasting life.

The smooth texture of the metal, its shine, and the ease with which it can be worked to convey a delicate effect or a strong visual impact have inspired artists throughout the centuries. An ounce of gold can be beaten out to 300 square feet (about twenty-eight square metres). The metal is so soft that it can be hammered cold by primitive goldsmiths and worked by more skilled craftsmen into the most intricate designs. Gold jewellery and ornaments soon became the visible evidence of riches, as they are today. Even in the world of popular music, gold is associated with significant wealth, even though a coveted golden disc may contain only 0·03 grams of gold. And an Olympic gold medal is still the ultimate goal of the athlete.

Jewellery remains the principal use of gold today. Most of the gold used for this purpose is alloyed with silver, copper and zinc to produce various shades of yellow gold, or with nickel, copper and zinc to produce white gold. Most of this gold is of 14 carat quality, a carat representing a measure of purity on a scale of 1 to 24. Fourteen carat gold therefore contains 14/24ths or 58·35 per cent pure gold.

The industrial use of the metal is rapidly increasing, particularly in the electronics industries. Gold is a superb reflector of light and heat, and the metal is used to insulate delicate instruments from excessive temperatures and to provide heat-reflecting surfaces for window glass and protective shields for aircraft. It is an excellent conductor of electricity, too, and a microscopic circuit of liquid gold can replace miles of wiring in a computer. It is applied as a finish to electrical connectors and as a thin coating in telephone relay systems. It is also used in the manufacture of transistors and microelectronic assemblies. Gold is widely used in dentistry and for decorating china and glassware. In 1977 a gold-plated Rolls-Royce was sold to a wealthy businessman for £83,500.

The metal is widely distributed over the earth's surface in veins, often in association with quartz, and as alluvial deposits in which gold has been separated from other minerals and become concentrated in streams or sediments. Tiny grains of gold are often carried long distances by streams and can be recovered by panning. Yet, despite its wide distribution, gold is still scarce enough for its value to remain extremely high. About 60 per cent of all the gold mined to date is held by governments and central banks where it is used to support the paper currencies of individual nations and as the most reliable method of international payment.

Today most of the world's gold comes from South Africa, which produced 67·4 per cent of the gold found in 1969, followed by Canada (13·9 per cent) and Russia (13·5 per cent). But significant quantities of gold are still produced throughout the world, from Ghana to the Philippines and Colombia to Fiji. The greatest consumers of gold are the United States, Europe, India and Pakistan. These countries use most of it to make jewellery, but a significant proportion is used for electronic and dental purposes, especially in the United States.

It has been estimated that the total amount of gold extracted from the earth's surface during the last five hundred years could be contained in a cube measuring fifteen yards (fourteen metres) in each direction. People have died and nations have been humbled to obtain this seemingly small amount. The story of the hunt for this gold is a long and violent one; it has taken place in many parts of the world and at all periods in history. This book does not attempt to tell the entire story – only parts of it. But it provides a glimpse of some of the most exciting and colourful incidents in the story, and of some of the extraordinary people whose desire for gold led them to risk their lives in order to possess it.

2. Gold of the gods

The child of Zeus

The desire for limitless wealth has brought misfortune and unhappiness to innumerable people in history and in legend. To the peoples of the ancient world gold was inextricably linked with the gods. 'Gold is the child of Zeus,' wrote the Greek poet Pindar. 'Neither moth nor rust devoureth it; but the mind of man is devoured by this supreme possession.' Ancient legends continually associate gold with the gods; the metal was immortal as they were, and the same colour as the sun which gave life to all. In the hands of wise men, guided by the gods, gold could be a blessing; but if men ignored divine advice and thought only of their own avarice, gold could bring only unhappiness.

Midas, king of the Phrygians, is the supreme example of a foolish mortal whose desire for gold brought him nothing but discomfort. In Book XI of *The Metamorphoses*, Ovid tells the story of the Phrygian king who is granted a wish by the god Bacchus as a reward for returning his drunken tutor to him:

The god was glad to have his tutor back, and in return gave Midas the right to choose himself a gift – a privilege which Midas welcomed, but one which did him little good, for he was fated to make poor use of the opportunity he was given. He said to the god: 'Grant that whatever my person touches be turned to yellow gold.' Bacchus, though sorry that Midas had not asked for something better, granted his request, and presented him with this baneful gift. The Phrygian king went off cheerfully, delighted with the misfortune which had befallen him. He tested the good faith of Bacchus' promise by touching this and that, and could scarcely believe his own senses when he broke a green twig from a low-growing branch of oak, and the twig turned to gold. He lifted a stone from the ground and the stone, likewise, gleamed pale gold. He touched a sod of earth and the earth, by the power of his touch, became a lump of ore. The dry ears of corn which he gathered were a harvest of golden metal, and when he plucked an apple from a tree and held it in his hand, you would have thought that the Hesperides had given it to him. If he laid his finger on the pillars of his lofty doorways, they were seen to shine and glitter, and even when he washed his hands in clear water, the trickles that flowed over his palms might have served to deceive Danaë. He dreamed of everything turned to gold, and his hopes soared beyond the limits of his imagination.
So he exulted in his good fortune, while servants set before him tables piled high with meats, and with bread in abundance. But then, when he touched a piece of bread, it grew stiff and hard: if he hungrily tried to bite into the meat, a sheet of gold encased the food, as soon as his teeth came in contact with it. He took some wine, itself the discovery of the god who had endowed him with his power, and adding clear water, mixed himself a drink: the liquid could be seen turning to molten gold as it passed his lips.

Wretched in spite of his riches, dismayed by the strange disaster which had befallen him, Midas prayed for a way of escape from his wealth, loathing what he had lately desired. No amount of food could relieve his hunger, parching thirst burned his throat, and he was tortured, as he deserved, by the gold he now hated. Raising his shining arms, he stretched his hands to heaven and cried: 'Forgive me, father Bacchus! I have sinned, yet pity me, I pray, and save me speedily from this disaster that promised so fair!' The gods are kind: when Midas confessed his fault, Bacchus restored him to his former state, cancelling the gift which, in fulfilment of his promise, he had given the king. 'And now,' he said, 'to rid yourself of the remaining traces of that gold which you so foolishly desired, go to the river close by the great city of Sardis. Then make your way along the Lydian ridge, travelling upstream till you come to the water's source. There, where the foaming spring bubbles up in great abundance, plunge your head and body in the water and, at the same time, wash away your crime.' The king went to the spring as he was bidden: his power to change things into gold passed from his person into the stream, and coloured its water. Even today, though the vein of ore is now so ancient, the soil of the fields is hardened by the grains it receives, and gleams with gold where the water from the river moistens its sods.

The story of Midas belongs to legend and not to history, but Ovid places the stream where Midas washed in Lydia, the country in Asia Minor once ruled by Croesus, a king forever associated with enormous wealth. Lydia was rich in gold and attracted the attention of the Persians during their conquests in the sixth century BC. Croesus sensed that attack was imminent and travelled to the shrine of Apollo in Delphi to seek the advice of the Oracle there. His offerings to the shrine were recorded by Herodotus in his *Histories*, an account which provides impressive evidence of the extent of Croesus' wealth, and of his generosity:

Croesus now attempted to win the favour of the Delphian Apollo by a magnificent sacrifice. Of every kind of appropriate animal he slaughtered three thousand; he burnt in a huge pile a number of precious objects – couches overlaid with gold or silver, golden cups, tunics, and other richly coloured garments – in the hope of binding the god more closely to his interest; and he issued a command that every Lydian was also to offer a sacrifice according to his means. After this ceremony he melted down an enormous quantity of gold into one hundred and seventeen ingots about eighteen inches long, nine inches wide, and three inches thick; four of the ingots were of refined gold weighing approximately a hundred and forty-two pounds each: the rest were alloyed and weighed about a hundred and fourteen pounds. He also caused the image of a lion to be made of refined gold, in weight some five hundred and seventy pounds. This statue, when the temple at Delphi was burnt down, fell from the gold bricks which formed its base and lives today in the Corinthian treasury. It lost about two hundred pounds weight in the fire, and now weighs only three hundred and seventy pounds.

This was by no means all that Croesus sent to Delphi; there were also two huge mixing-bowls, one of gold which was placed on the right-hand side of the entrance to the temple, the other of silver, on the left. These also were moved at the time of the fire, and the golden one, which weighs nearly a quarter of a ton, now stands in the treasury of the Clazomenians... There were many other gifts of no great importance, including round silver basins; but I must not forget to mention a figure of a woman, in gold, four and a half feet high, said by the Delphians to represent the woman who baked Croesus' bread. Lastly, he sent his own wife's necklaces and girdles. These, then, were the offerings which Croesus sent to Delphi; to the shrine of Amphiaraus, the story of whose valour and misfortune he knew, he sent a shield of solid gold and a spear, also of solid gold throughout, both shaft and head; the shield and spear were still at Thebes in my own day, in the temple of Ismenian Apollo.

It was only to be expected that the grateful Oracle should give Croesus the advice that he needed, but, this time, its prophecy was wrong: the Persians conquered Lydia and added its gold to their rapidly increasing wealth. Croesus is remembered now for more than his fabulous riches: it was he who invented and established the first system of gold and silver coinage.

Ants, griffins and one-eyed men

The ancient chroniclers have left us ample detail of the wealth of their kings, but they are less expansive on the source of the gold which adorned their palaces. Solomon, we are told in the Book of Kings, was fortunate enough to have an annual income of 'six hundred threescore and six talents of gold' in addition to the 'traffick of the spice merchants, and of all the kings of Arabia, and of the governors of the country'. This figure presumably did not include the cargo of the navy of Tharshish, which brought him, once every three years, 'gold and silver, ivory, and apes, and peacocks', or, for that matter, such unexpected windfalls as the mere hundred

Gold of the gods

and twenty talents of gold brought by the visiting Queen of Sheba, and the cargo of gold from Ophir donated by the navy of Hiram. It has been estimated that the minimum equivalent weight of a talent was about sixty pounds (twenty-seven kilograms); little wonder, then, that Solomon 'exceeded all the kings of the earth for riches'.

These riches, though, were won at the expense of much misery and hardship. Gold had to be prospected and mined by the subject peoples of kings like Croesus and Solomon, and they did not share in the subsequent prosperity of their rulers. Contemporary accounts of mining methods offer an entertaining mixture of fact and fantasy. Herodotus, who liked to believe the tall stories he was told, scoffed at the idea of one source of gold:

It is clear that it is the northern parts of Europe which are richest in gold, but how it is procured is another mystery. The story goes that the one-eyed Arimaspians steal it from the griffins who guard it; personally, however, I refuse to believe in one-eyed men who in other respects are like the rest of us.

Herodotus may not have accepted the one-eyed Arimaspians but he does seem to have believed the story of the ants of Pactyica:

There are other Indians further north, round the city of Caspatyrus and in the country of Pactyica, who in their mode of life resemble the Bactrians. These are the most warlike of the Indian tribes, and it is they who go out to fetch the gold – for in this region there is a sandy desert. There is found in this desert a kind of ant of great size – bigger than a fox, though not so big as a dog. Some specimens, which were caught there, are

Gold coins of the Sassanian dynasty of Persia (AD 224–651)

Gold and Gold-Hunters

kept at the palace of the Persian king. These creatures as they burrow underground throw up the sand in heaps, just as our own ants throw up the earth, and they are very like ours in shape. The sand has a rich content of gold, and this it is that the Indians are after when they make their expeditions into the desert. Each man harnesses three camels abreast, a female, on which he rides, in the middle, and a male on each side on a leading-rein, and takes care that the female is one who has as recently as possible dropped her young. Their camels are as fast as horses, and much more powerful carriers ... That, then, is how these Indians equip themselves for the expedition, and they plan their timetable so as actually to get their hands on the gold during the hottest part of the day, when the heat will have driven the ants underground ... When the Indians reach the place where the gold is, they fill the bags they have brought with them with sand, and start for home again as fast as they can go; for the ants (if we may believe the Persians' story) smell them and at once give chase; nothing in the world can touch these ants for speed, so not one of the Indians would get home alive, if they did not make sure of a good start while the ants were mustering their forces. The male camels, who are slower movers than the females, soon begin to drag and are left behind, one after the other, while the females are kept going hard by the memory of their young, who were left at home.

According to the Persians, most of the gold is got in the way I have described; they also mine a certain quantity – but not so much – within their own territory.

A more circumstantial and accurate account of early mining methods is given by Diodorus of Sicily, who wrote a history of the world in forty volumes during the first century BC. His style is not as lively as that of Herodotus, but his description of the gold mines of Egypt and of the lives of the miners who worked them has the ring of truth:

At the extremity of Egypt and in the contiguous territory of both Arabia and Ethiopia there lies a region which contains many large gold mines, where the gold is secured in great quantities with much suffering and at great expense ... For the kings of Egypt gather together and condemn to the mining of the gold such as have been found guilty of some crime and captives of war, as well as those who have been accused unjustly and thrown into prison because of their anger, and occasionally all their relatives as well, by this means not only inflicting punishment upon those found guilty but also securing at the same time great revenues from their labours. And those who have been condemned in this way – and they are a great multitude and are all bound in chains – work at their task unceasingly both by day and throughout the entire night, enjoying no respite and being carefully cut off from any means of escape; since guards of foreign soldiers who speak a language different from theirs stand watch over them, so that not a man ... is able to corrupt one of his keepers.

The gold-bearing earth which is hardest they first burn with a hot fire, and when they have crumbled it in this way they continue the working of it by hand; and the soft rock which can yield to moderate effort is crushed with a sledge by myriads of unfortunate wretches. And the entire operations are in charge of a skilled worker who distinguishes the stone and points it out to the labourers; and of those who are assigned to this unfortunate task the physically strongest break the quartz-rock with iron hammers, applying no skill to the task, but only force, and cutting tunnels through the stone, not in a straight line but wherever the seam of gleaming rock may lead. Now these men, working in darkness as they do because of the bending and winding of the passages, carry lamps bound on their foreheads; and since much of the time they change the position of their bodies to follow the particular character of the stone they throw the blocks, as they cut them out, on the ground; and at this

Gold of the gods

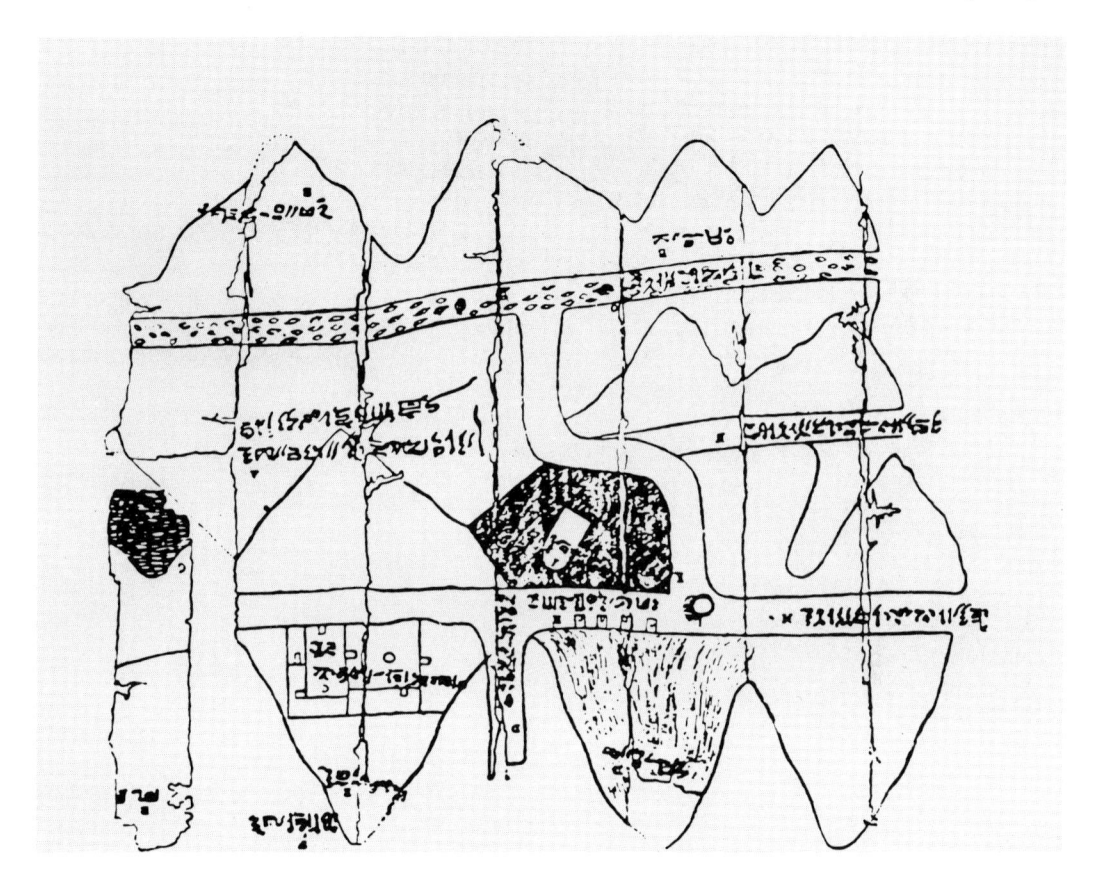

Map of an Egyptian gold mine, 1320 BC. This is the world's oldest existing map

task they labour without ceasing beneath the sternness and blows of an overseer.

The boys there who have not yet come to maturity, entering through the tunnels into the galleries formed by the removal of the rock, laboriously gather up the rock as it is cast down piece by piece and carry it out into the open to the place outside the entrance. Then those who are above thirty years of age take this quarried stone from them and with iron pestles pound a specified amount of it in stone mortars, until they have worked it down to the size of vetch. Thereupon the women and older men receive from them the rock of this size and cast it into mills of which a number stand there in a row, and taking their places in groups of two or three at the spoke or handle of each mill they grind it until they have worked down the amount given them to the consistency of the finest flour ... No leniency or respite of any kind is given to any man who is sick, or maimed, or aged, or in the case of a woman for her weakness, but all without exception are compelled by blows to persevere in their labours, until through ill-treatment they die in the midst of their tortures. Consequently the poor unfortunates believe, because their punishment is so excessively severe, that the future will always be more terrible than the present and therefore look forward to death as more to be desired than life.

In the last steps the skilled workmen receive the stone which has been ground to powder and take it off for its complete and final working, for they rub the marble which has been worked down upon a broad board which is slightly inclined, pouring water over it all the while; whereupon the earthy matter in it, melted away by the action of the water, runs down the inclined board, while that which contains the gold remains on the wood because of its weight. And repeating this a number of times, they first of all rub it gently with their hands, and then lightly pressing it with sponges of loose texture they remove in this way whatever is porous and earthy, until there remains only pure gold-dust. Then at last other skilled workmen take what has been recovered and put it by fixed measure and weight into earthen jars, mixing with it a lump of lead proportionate to the mass, lumps of salt and a little tin, and adding thereto barley bran; thereupon they put on it a close-fitting lid, and smearing it over carefully with mud they bake it in a kiln for five successive days and as many nights; and at the end of this period, when they have let the jars cool off, of the other matter they find no remains in the jars, but the gold they recover in pure form, there being but little waste.

3. The gold makers

There has never been enough gold to satisfy man's desire for it and before long he turned his inventive genius towards the search for methods of producing gold by transmuting baser metals. Alchemists, as they were called, flourished in the East and in Arabia before the birth of Christ, and the mystery and magic which shrouded their researches continued to intrigue and excite man's imagination throughout the Middle Ages and beyond, as knowledge of alchemical methods spread into Europe.

The principal aim of the alchemist was to find the Philosopher's Stone, a mysterious agent which possessed the properties of producing gold and prolonging life. The possession of gold and eternal life have always

Above: *A sixteenth-century alchemist's laboratory*

Gold and Gold-Hunters

A noble medicine

Although the finder of the Philosopher's Stone would have thought twice before broadcasting his discovery to the world, many alchemical treatises and studies were written during the Middle Ages. This was a time when the practice of alchemy was at its height and when, more than ever before, public imagination was stimulated and excited by the activities of the alchemists. One of the best-known practitioners of the time was Basil Valentinus, an obscure figure who published a number of scientific works. In *The Great Stone of the Philosophers*, he offered a useful recipe for the elusive Stone:

Take the very best gold you can have, One Part; and of good Hungarian antimony, Six Parts. Melt these together upon a fire and pour it out into such a pot as the goldsmiths use. It then becomes a Regulus. This Regulus is to be again melted, and the antimony separated from it. Then add mercury, and melt it again. Do this three times. Then beat the gold very thin, and make an amalgam with more quicksilver. Let the quicksilver fume away over a gentle fire till nothing remain but gold. Then take One Part of saltpetre and One Part of sal ammoniac and half as much of pebbles well washed. Mix them, and distil in an earthen retort in a furnace.

The fluid is then mixed with the prepared calx of gold, and water added. Digest it in warm ashes at a gentle heat for Fourteen Days. Add water again, distil and redistil until the gold comes over. To this spiritualized solution of gold, rain water is added, and Three Parts of mercury. Decant the water and dry the amalgam, drive off

dominated man's ambition, and the possession of the Stone which would conveniently satisfy both these desires became the overriding obsession of the alchemist. Their researches were cloaked in elaborate ritual and they jealously guarded their secrets. After all, whoever discovered the Stone would possess ultimate power: unlimited wealth and influence would be his to command.

Thomas Norton was a very famous fifteenth-century alchemist, who wrote an Ordinal of Alchimy. *This picture shows him in his laboratory. Notice the balance in a glass case and the symbols for gold and silver on the table*

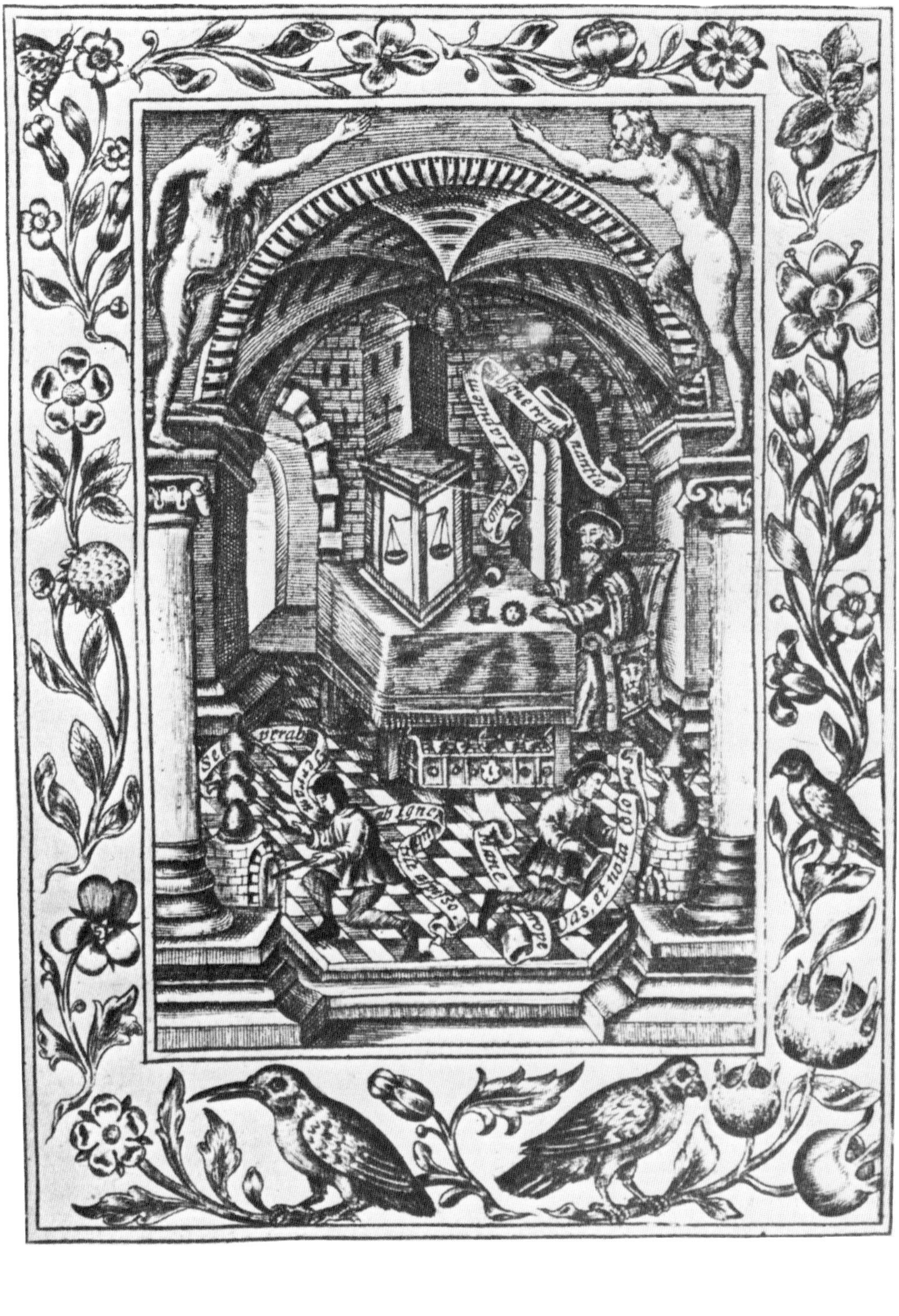

the quicksilver, and there will remain a very fair powder, of a purple colour. Then must be made the Tartar of the Philosophers from the ashes of the vine and make a strong lee with it to coagulation. There remains a reddish matter, which must be dissolved in spirit of wine. Then take the other part of mercury of pure gold and pour on and distil. The precipitated mercury and the oyl of gold are then to be mixed, placed in a hermetically sealed glass and put into a threefold furnace and allowed to putrefy for a month and become quite black.

Increase the fire, and the blackness will vanish. It changes to many colours. Increase it to the fourth degree, and the glass will look like silver; to the fifth degree, and it becomes like gold. Continue this, and you will see your Matter lye beneath like a brown oyl, which at length becomes dry like granite.

He that obtains this, may render thanks to God, for poverty will forsake him; for this noble medicine is such a Stone to which nothing in the world may be compared for virtue, riches and power. If this medicine, after being fermented with other pure gold, doth likewise tinge many thousand parts of all other metals into very good gold, such gold likewise becometh a penetrate medicine, that one part thereof will transmute a thousand parts of other metals, and much more beyond belief, into perfect gold.

The mysterious visitor

It is hardly surprising that the attention of charlatans and confidence tricksters should have been quickly turned towards alchemy and the spurious alchemist was often able to persuade his victims that the secret of the Philosopher's Stone was his – and could be theirs too, for a price. The easiest trick was to secrete a piece of real gold into a crucible, perhaps inside a cube of charcoal. The heat in the crucible would release the gold, astonishing and convincing the audience.

It is easy enough to criticize the work and ideas of the alchemists, and tempting to dismiss them as either misguided fools, blinded by dreams of wealth and power, or else as outright crooks, intent on deceiving the gullible for gain. There is no proof that any alchemist succeeded in making gold, but there are cases which lead one to wonder.

One of the most believable accounts is by Johann Friedrich Schweitzer, more generally known as Helvetius, a sober and respected Swiss doctor who was Court Physician to the Prince of Orange. He was a man of culture and discernment, and the author of many serious medical and botanical studies. His own story of his first contact with an alchemist, and of his conversion to the practice of the art, has been dissected and discussed by generations of doubters, none of whom has yet been able to discover any loophole in the account:

The twenty-seventh of December, 1666, in the afternoon, came a Stranger to my house at The Hague, in a plebeian habit, honest gravity, and serious authority; of a mean stature, a little long face, with a few small pock holes, and most black hair, not at all curled, a beardless chin, about three or four and forty years of age (as I guessed) and born in North Holland. After salutation he beseeched me with a great reverence to pardon his rude accesses, being a great lover of the Pyrotechnian Art; adding, he formerly endeavoured to visit me with a friend of his, and told me that he had read some of my small treatises ...

After other large discourse of experiments in metals this Elias asked me if I could know the philosopher's stone when I saw it. I answered not at all, though I had read much of it in Paracelsus, Helmont, Basilius, and others; yet I dare not say I could know the philosopher's matter. In the interim he took out of his bosom pouch or pocket, a cunningly worked ivory box, and out of it took three ponderous pieces or small lumps of the stone, each about the bigness of a small walnut, transparent, of a pale brimstone colour, whereunto did stick the internal scales of the crucible, wherein it appeared this most noble substance was melted; they might be judged able to produce about twenty tons of gold, which when I had greedily seen and handled almost a quarter of an hour, and drawn from the owner many rare secrets of its admirable effects in human and metallic bodies, and other magical properties, I returned him this treasure of treasures; truly with a most sorrowful mind, after the custom of those who conquer themselves, yet (as was but just) very thankfully and humbly. I further desired to know why the colour was yellow, and not red, ruby colour, or purple, as philosophers write; he answered, that was nothing, for the matter was mature and ripe enough.

Then I humbly requested him to bestow a little piece of the medicine on me, in perpetual memory of him, though but the quantity of a coriander or hemp seed. He presently answered, O no, no, this is not lawful though thou wouldst give me as many ducats in gold as would fill this room, not for the value of the matter, but for some particular consequences not lawful to divulge, nay, if it were possible (said he) that fire could be burnt of fire, I would rather at this instant cast all this substance into the fiercest flames.

... I earnestly craved but a most small crumb or parcel of his powder or stone, to transmute four grains of lead to gold; and at last out of his philosophical commiseration, he gave me a crumb as big as a rape or turnip seed; saying, receive this small parcel of the greatest treasure of the world, which truly few kings or princes have ever known or seen. But I said, this perhaps will not transmute four grains of lead, whereupon he bid me deliver it him back, which in hopes of a greater parcel I did; but he cutting halfe off with his nail, flung it into the fire, and gave me the rest neatly wrapped in blue paper ... So I gave him great thanks for my diminished Treasure, concentrated truly in the superlative degree, and put the same charily up into my little box; saying I meant to try it the next day; nor would I reveal it to any.

The mysterious visitor then took his leave, promising to return the next day. But he did not come back and Helvetius never saw him again.

Helvetius thought no more of the visitor's gift; the man's failure to return had made him doubt his story altogether. But Helvetius' wife, more curious than he, persuaded him to see whether the stranger's gift would, in fact, make gold:

I commanded a fire to be made (thinking alas) ... I fear indeed this man hath deluded me; nevertheless my wife wrapped the said matter in wax, and cut half an ounce or six drams of old lead, and put it into a crucible in the fire, which being melted, my wife put in the said Medicine made up into a small pill or button, which presently made such a hissing and bubbling in its perfect operation, that within a quarter of an hour all the mass of lead was totally transmuted into the best and finest gold, which made us amazed as planet-struck.

And indeed (had I lived in Ovid's age) there could not have been a rarer metamorphosis than this, by the art of alchemy. Yea, could I have enjoyed Argus's eyes, with a hundred more, I could not sufficiently gaze upon this so admirable and almost miraculous a work of nature; for this melted lead (after projection) shewed us on the fire the rarest and most beautiful colours imaginable; yea, and the greenest colour, which as soon as poured forth into an ingot, it got the lively fresh colour of blood; and being cold shined as the purest and most refined resplendent gold. Truly I, and all standing about me, were exceedingly startled, and did run with this aurified lead (being yet hot) unto the goldsmith, who wondered at the fineness, and after a short trial of touch, he judg'd it the most excellent gold in the whole world, and offered to give most willingly fifty florins for every ounce of it.

It is a strange story but a convincing one. No one has been able to disprove it, and alchemical historians have been puzzled by it ever since the account was published. Was Helvetius the victim of a skilful confidence trick? Or had the mysterious stranger really discovered the Philosopher's Stone? We shall probably never know.

Christopher Columbus

4. Gold of the New World

Gold is most excellent

Many of the world's greatest discoveries have been made by accident, and one of the most significant of these was Christopher Columbus' landing in the New World in 1492. His intention had been to sail westwards to Asia and establish a new trading route from Spain to the Orient; to the last, Columbus seems to have been convinced that the islands of the West Indies were the Orient: he assumed that the island of Hispaniola was Japan and that Cuba was the 'extreme edge of the East'. These illusions may have been deliberately fostered in order to gain further support for his explorations: his royal employers, Ferdinand and Isabella, were expecting results and Columbus was anxious to justify his theories. His letters and reports to his sovereigns are therefore often rather sad, filled as they are with accounts of the great quantities of gold to be discovered on the *next* island, and of regions of wealth in the domains of *neighbouring* chiefs. In July 1503, Columbus wrote as follows to the king and queen during his fourth and final voyage:

Most serene, exalted and mighty King and Queen our sovereigns: I crossed from Cadiz to the Canary Islands in four days, and thence to the Indies in sixteen, where I wrote that my intention was to hasten my voyage while I had good ships, crews and provisions, and that my course was for the island of Jamaica, and at the island of Dominica I wrote this. Till I reached there I had as good weather as I could have wished for, but the night of my arrival there was a great storm, and I have been dogged by bad weather ever since ...

I reached the land of Cariay [Nicaragua], where I stayed to repair the ships, replenish the stores and rest the crews, who had become very weak. I had myself, as I have said, several times come near to death. Here I received news of the goldfields in the province of Ciamba which I was seeking. Two Indians brought me to Carambaru, where the people go naked, wearing shining gold discs round their necks, but they would not sell or barter them.

They gave me the names of many places on the sea-coast where they said there was gold and goldfields too. The last of these was Veragua, about twenty leagues away. I set out with the intention of inspecting them all, but when I was half-way there I learnt that there were other goldfields only two days' journey away, and decided to send and inspect these. The expedition was to have left on the Eve of St Simon and St Jude, but such seas and winds arose that night that we had to run before it and the Indian who was to have guided us to the goldfields remained on board.

In all these places I had visited, I had found the information given me true, and this assured me that the same would be so of the province of Ciguare, which, as they told me, lies inland nine days' journey westward. They say that there is a vast quantity of gold there and that the people wear coral ornaments on their heads and stout bracelets of the same material on their wrists and ankles. They also embellish and inlay stools, chests and tables with it. I was told too that the

Gold and Gold-Hunters

women wore circlets on their heads that hung down to their shoulders. All the people of these parts agree about this and from all that they say I should be glad of a tenth of those riches. According to reports they are all acquainted with red pepper.

In Ciguare the custom is to trade in fairs and markets, and I was shown this people's method of trading. It was also said that their ships carry cannon, bows and arrows, swords and shields, and that they wear clothes and that there are horses in that country. It was said that these people wage war, wear rich clothing and have good houses. They say also that Ciguare is surrounded by water, and that ten days' journey away is the river Ganges ...

As I said, on the Eve of St Simon and St Jude, I ran where the wind carried me, and could not resist it. I sheltered in a harbour from the great violence of sea and storm and decided there not to turn back to the goldfields, but left them, considering them gained already. I set out to continue my voyage in rain and reach the harbour of Bastimentos, into which I was driven against my will. Storm and the strong current held me there for fourteen days and when I finally left it was in bad weather. Having with difficulty made fifteen leagues, I was driven back by the furious wind and current to the port which I had just left ... I stayed there fifteen days, compelled to do so by the cruel weather, and when I thought that it was ending I found it was only beginning. So I decided not to go to the goldfields or do anything else until the weather should be favourable for me to set out and put to sea ...

On the day of Epiphany (6 January) I

Gold of the New World

reached Veragua, completely broken in spirit. Here Our Lord gave me a river and a safe harbour, although it was less than eight feet deep. I got in with difficulty and next day the storm returned. If it had found me outside I should not have been able to get in because of the bar. It rained without stopping until 14 February, so I never had an opportunity of exploring the country or of repairing my condition in any way. On 24 January, when I was lying there in safety, the river suddenly became very high and violent. The cables and bollards were broken and the ships were almost swept away. I had never seen them in greater danger, but Our Lord saved us as ever. I know of no one who has suffered greater trials.

On 6 February, when it was still raining, I sent seventy men inland and at five leagues away they found many goldfields. The Indians whom they had with them led them to a very high hill and from there showed them all the surrounding country as far as the eye could reach, saying that there was gold everywhere and that there were goldfields twenty days' journey to the west. They named the towns and villages and showed where they lay thickest or thinnest. I afterwards learned that the chief who had given us these Indians had told them to point to distant goldfields which belonged to a rival chieftain, though within his own territory a man could collect a full load of gold in ten days whenever he wished.

I have with me these Indians who were his servants, and they will bear witness to this. The boats went to the place where his township lay, and my brother returned with his men all carrying the gold they had gathered in the four hours

Ancient gold washing at Santo Domingo

they had been ashore. The quantity must be great, since none of them had ever seen goldfields and most of them had never seen unrefined gold before ...

When I discovered the Indies I said that they were the richest domain in the whole world in respect of gold, pearls, precious stones, spices, and trade and markets, and because all these things were not produced at once I was subjected to abuse. Because of this ill-treatment I now report nothing except that which I learnt from the natives of the land. One thing I dare say, since there are so many witnesses to it, and this is that in the land of Veragua I saw more evidences of gold in the first two days than in four years in Hispaniola, that the lands hereabouts could not be more beautiful or better cultivated, that the people could not be more timid, and that there is a fine harbour, a lovely river, which could be defended against the world. All this makes for the safety of the Christians, and their security of possession, and also offers great hopes of honour and expansion to the Christian faith. The voyage there will be as short as that to Hispaniola, since it can be made with a following wind. Your Highnesses are as much lords of this country as you are of Jerez or Toledo. Your ships can come here as safely as if they still lay at home. They will bring back gold from here, whereas if they wish to take the products of other lands they would have to take it by force or come back empty-handed, and inland they must entrust themselves to savages.

Concerning the other things of which I have refrained from speaking I have given the reasons for my reticence. I have not stated the sixth part of what I have learnt in all that I have said and written, nor do I swear to it, nor do I claim to have reached the fountain-head. The Genoese, Venetians and all other people who have pearls, precious stones and other valuables take them to the ends of the world to sell and turn into gold. Gold is most excellent. Gold constitutes treasure, and anyone who has it can do whatever he likes in the world. With it he can succeed in bringing souls to paradise. When the people of these lands in the district of Veragua die, their gold is buried with their bodies, or so it is said.

Solomon was brought 666 talents of gold from a single expedition, in addition to what he received from merchants and sailors and his payments from Arabia. With this gold he made 200 lances and 300 shields, and the overlay of his throne, which was of solid gold adorned with precious stones; also many other objects and great vessels inlaid with jewels. Josephus writes of this in his chronicle of *Antiquities*, and it is also mentioned in the Book of Chronicles and the Book of Kings. Josephus believes that this gold came from Aurea. If this is so, the goldfields of Aurea are in my opinion the same as these of Veragua, which, as I have said, extend twenty days' journey westwards, and are everywhere the same distance from the Pole and the Equator. Solomon bought all this gold, precious stones and silver, but your Majesties may send orders for them to be collected at your pleasure. David, in his will, left 3000 talents of gold from the Indies to Solomon to help in the building of the Temple, and according to Josephus it came from these same lands ...

Although I have information that the gold belonging to the chief of Veragua and the chiefs of the surrounding districts is very abundant, I do not think it would be well, or to your Highnesses' advantage, for it to be seized by way of plunder. Fair dealing will prevent scandal and disrepute, and bring this gold into the treasury down to the last grain.

Given a month of good weather, I could complete my whole voyage. Being short of ships I have not delayed any longer but resumed my journey. I trust in my Creator that I shall be of service to your Highnesses in every respect, so long as my health lasts ... I rate this trade and the possession of these extensive goldfields more highly than anything else we have achieved in the Indies ...

Written in the Indies on the island of Jamaica, 7 July 1503.

The tears of the sun

The news of Columbus' discoveries and the evidence of the riches of the Indies which he brought back to his rulers excited Spanish interest in the new lands. Further expeditions set sail to colonize the territory already claimed for Spain and to uncover the wealth of gold rumoured to lie in the hinterland of central America. The instructions of King Ferdinand were plain: 'Get gold, humanely if you can, but at all hazards get gold.' Humanity was to play little part in the search!

Hernando Cortés first set sail for the Indies in 1504 where he established himself as an influential citizen of Cuba. In 1518 he sailed for the mainland, determined to find the lands of gold. He and his companions landed near Vera Cruz, and learned for the first time of the inland country of Mexico and of the Aztec civilization there. The Aztec king Montezuma sent gifts and words of welcome to Cortés, and the Spaniards pressed on towards Mexico, anxious to lay their hands on the vast stores of gold which they now knew existed in the Aztec capital. Gold was of little value to the Aztecs except as decoration, and if the possession of it would placate the pale invaders, Montezuma was prepared to give it freely. But there was another reason why the king allowed Cortés and his small force of men to advance unchecked on his capital: Aztec myth foretold the return to earth of the great god Quetzalcoatl. Was Cortés an emissary from the god? Montezuma was not prepared to take any chances. And he was astute enough to realize that Cortés was merely the forerunner of a greater invasion and that the survival of his nation might well depend on his kind treatment of the new arrivals.

Montezuma's capital, Mexico-Tenochtitlan, astonished the Spanish when they eventually reached it. They were dazzled by the wealth of the island city and by the lavish gifts of gold and precious stones which Montezuma showered on them. Montezuma surrendered himself to Cortés, becoming a vassal of the king of Spain, and the Spanish triumph was complete. But when Montezuma's brother launched an attack on the Spaniards the king was killed in the fighting that followed and Cortés was forced to withdraw from the capital, taking his gold with him. But this was only a temporary setback to Spanish ambition. By 1521 the Aztecs were finally conquered, and Mexico – with all its gold – became part of the Spanish empire.

Far to the south of Mexico, in the vertical landscape of Peru, lay the kingdom of the

Incas. Rumours of the wealth of this country and of the immense stores of gold held by the king soon filtered northwards and reached the eager ears of the Spanish who, by now, had crossed to the Pacific and claimed that ocean in the name of Spain. An expedition led by Francisco Pizarro set out in 1526 to see whether the reports of this golden civilization were true.

Pizarro's discoveries in Peru exceeded his wildest expectations. Gold abounded in the Inca cities, and their sun temples were covered in golden ornament of the greatest beauty. The Incas worshipped the sun, and gold was inextricably linked with the god: they called it 'the tears wept by the sun'. Before long, the Inca king, Atahualpa, was captured by Pizarro at Caxamalca. The events of Atahualpa's captivity and of the days leading to his death are among the most extraordinary and tragic in the whole history of the Spanish conquest of America, a history that has seen more than its fair share of extraordinary and tragic events. The story has been superbly told by William H. Prescott in his classic *History of the Conquest of Peru*, first published in 1847. It remains the best account of the conquest, and subsequent archaeological discoveries have substantiated Prescott's narrative:

It was not long before Atahualpa discovered, amidst all the show of religious zeal in his Conquerors, a lurking appetite more potent in most of their bosoms than either religion or ambition. This was the love of gold. He determined to avail himself of it to procure his own freedom ...

In the hope, therefore, to effect his purpose by appealing to the avarice of his keepers, he one day told Pizarro that if he would set him free he would engage to cover the floor of the apartment on which they stood with gold. Those present listened with an incredulous smile; and as the Inca received no answer, he said, with some emphasis, that 'he would not merely cover the floor, but would fill the room with gold as high as he could reach'; and, standing on tiptoe, he stretched out his hand against the wall. All stared with amazement; while they regarded it as the insane boast of a man too eager to procure his liberty to weigh the meaning of his words. Yet Pizarro was sorely perplexed. As he had advanced into the country, much that he had seen, and all that he had heard, had confirmed the dazzling reports first received of the riches of Peru. Atahualpa himself had given him the most glowing picture of the wealth of the capital, where the roofs of the temples were plated with gold, while the walls were hung with tapestry and the floors inlaid with tiles of the same precious metal. There must be some foundation for all this. At all events, it was safe to accede to the Inca's proposition, since by so doing he could collect at once all the gold at his disposal, and thus prevent its being purloined or secreted by the natives. He therefore acquiesced in Atahualpa's offer, and, drawing a red line along the wall at the height which the Inca had indicated, he caused the terms of the proposal to be duly recorded by the notary. The apartment was about seventeen feet broad, by twenty-two feet long, and the line round the walls was nine feet from the floor. This space was to be filled with gold; but it was understood that the gold was not to be melted down into ingots, but to retain the original form of the articles into which it was manufactured, that the Inca might have the benefit of the space which they occupied. He further agreed to fill an adjoining room of smaller dimensions twice full with silver, in like manner; and he demanded two months to accomplish all this.

No sooner was this arrangement made than the Inca despatched couriers to Cuzco and the other principal places in the kingdom, with orders that the gold ornaments and utensils should be removed from the royal palaces, and

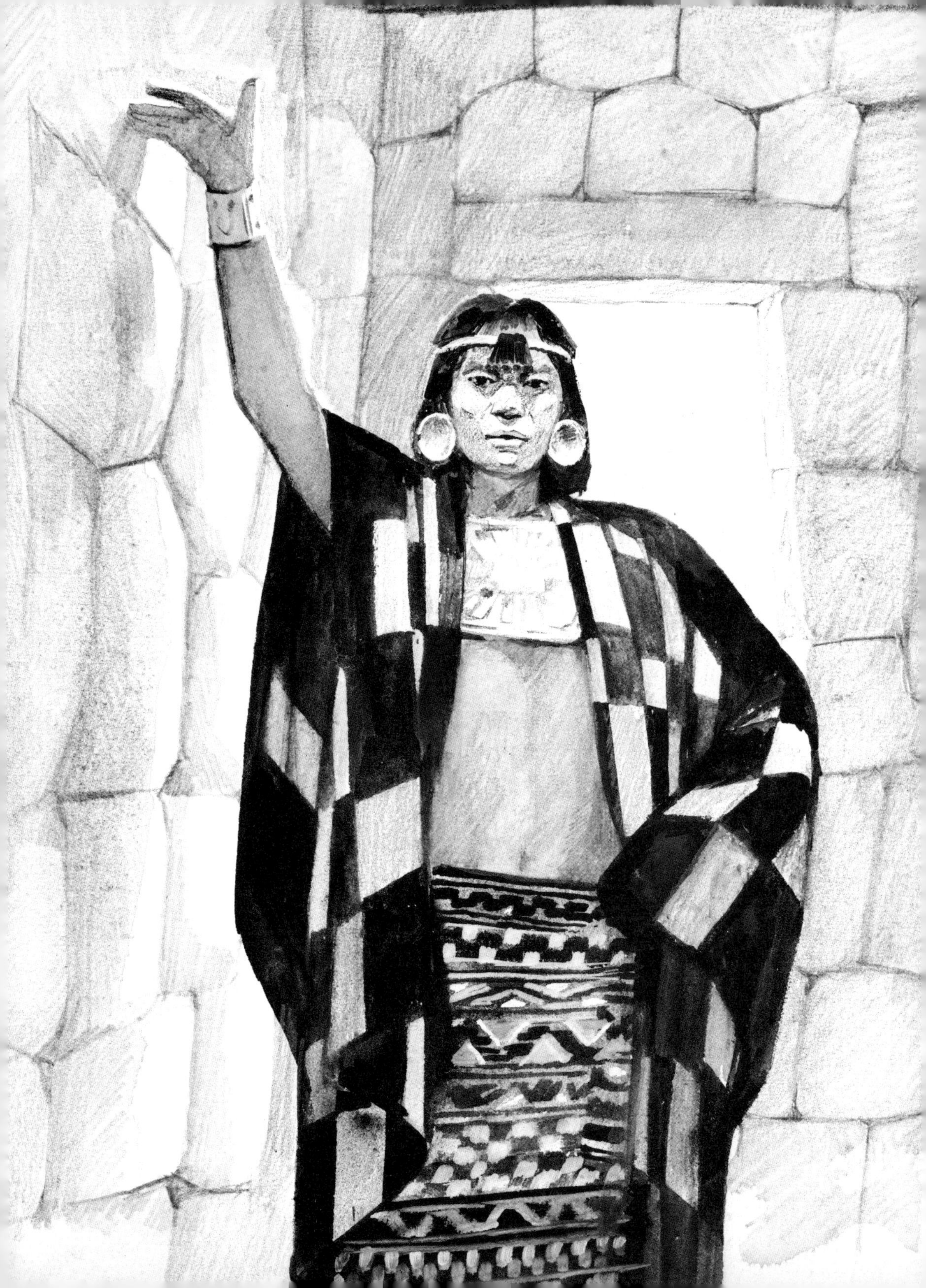

Gold of the New World

from the temples and other public buildings, and transported without loss of time to Caxamalca. Meanwhile he continued to live in the Spanish quarters, treated with the respect due to his rank, and enjoying all the freedom that was compatible with the security of his person ...

Several weeks had now passed since Atahualpa's emissaries had been despatched for the gold and silver that were to furnish his ransom to the Spaniards. But the distances were great, and the returns came in slowly. They consisted, for the most part, of massive pieces of plate, some of which weighed two or three *arrobas* – a Spanish weight of twenty-five pounds. On some days, articles of the value of thirty or forty thousand *pesos de oro* were brought in, and, occasionally, of the value of fifty or even sixty thousand *pesos*. The greedy eyes of the Conquerors gloated on the shining heaps of treasure, which were transported on the shoulders of the Indian porters, and, after being carefully registered, were placed in safe deposit under a strong guard. They now began to believe that the magnificent promises of the Inca would be fulfilled. But as their avarice was sharpened by the ravishing display of wealth such as they had hardly dared to imagine, they became more craving and impatient. They made no allowance for the distance and the difficulties of the way, and loudly inveighed against the tardiness with which the royal commands were executed. They even suspected Atahualpa of devising this scheme only to gain a pretext for communicating with his subjects in distant places, and of proceeding as dilatorily as possible, in order to secure time for the execution of his plans. Rumours of a rising among the Peruvians were circulated, and the Spaniards were in apprehension of some general and sudden assault on their quarters. Their new acquisitions gave them additional cause for solicitude: like a miser, they trembled in the midst of their treasures.

Pizarro reported to his captive the rumours

In Peru the Spaniards 'scoured the countryside for gold, making fantastic journeys across the mountains' – this picture comes from Relacion Historica del Viage a la America Meridional *(1748) by Jorge Juan and Antonio de Ulloa*

A street in Cuzco today

that were in circulation among the soldiers ... Atahualpa listened with undisguised astonishment, and indignantly repelled the charge, as false from beginning to end. 'No one of my subjects,' said he, 'would dare to appear in arms, or to raise his finger, without my orders. You have me,' he continued, 'in your power. Is not my life at your disposal? And what better security can you have for my fidelity?' He then represented to the Spanish commander that the distances of many of the places were very great; that to Cuzco, the capital, although a message might be sent by post, through a succession of couriers, in five days from Caxamalca, it would require weeks for a porter to travel over the same ground with a heavy load on his back. 'But, that you may be satisfied I am proceeding in good faith,' he added, 'I desire you will send some of your own people to Cuzco. I will give them a safe-conduct, and, when there, they can superintend the execution of the commission, and see with their own eyes that no hostile movements are intended.' It was a fair offer; and Pizarro, anxious to get more precise and authentic information of the state of the country, gladly availed himself of it ...

In the latter part of May, the three emissaries returned from Cuzco. They had been very successful in their mission. Owing to the Inca's order, and the awe which the white men now inspired throughout the country, the Spaniards had everywhere met with a kind reception ... Their accounts of the capital confirmed all that Pizarro had before heard of the wealth and population of the city. Though they had remained more than a week in this place, the emissaries had not seen the whole of it. The great temple of the Sun they found literally covered with plates of gold. They had entered the interior and beheld the royal mummies, seated each in his gold-embossed chair and in robes profusely covered with ornaments. The Spaniards had the grace to respect these, as they had been previously enjoined by the Inca; but they required that the plates which garnished the walls should be all removed. The Peruvians most reluctantly acquiesced in the commands of their sovereign to desecrate the national temple, which every inhabitant of the city regarded with peculiar pride and veneration. With less reluctance they assisted the Conquerors in stripping the ornaments from some of the other edifices, where the gold, however, being mixed with a large proportion of alloy, was of much less value.

The number of plates they tore from the temple of the Sun was seven hundred; and though of no great thickness, probably, they are compared in size to the lid of a chest ten or twelve inches wide. A cornice of pure gold encircled the edifice, but so strongly set in the stone that it fortunately defied the efforts of the spoilers. The Spaniards complained of the want of alacrity shown by the Indians in the work of destruction, and said that there were other parts of the city containing buildings rich in gold and silver which they had not been allowed to see. In truth, their mission, which at best was a most ungrateful one, had been rendered doubly annoying by the manner in which they had executed it. The emissaries were men of very low stamp, and puffed up by the honours conceded to them by the natives, they looked on themselves as entitled to these, and contemned the poor Indians as a race immeasurably beneath the European. They not only showed the most disgusting rapacity, but treated the highest nobles with wanton insolence. They even went so far, it is said, as to violate the privacy of the convents, and to outrage the religious sentiments of the Peruvians by their scandalous amours with the Virgins of the Sun. The people of Cuzco were so exasperated that they would have laid violent hands on them, but for their habitual reverence for the Inca, in whose name the Spaniards had come there. As it was, the Indians collected as much gold as was necessary to satisfy their unworthy visitors, and got rid of them as speedily as possible ...

The messengers brought with them, besides silver, full two hundred *cargas* or loads of gold. This was an important accession to the contributions of Atahualpa; and although the treasure was still considerably below the mark prescribed, the monarch saw with satisfaction the time drawing nearer for the completion of his ransom ...

The Spaniards had patiently waited till the return of the emissaries from Cuzco swelled the treasure to a large amount, though still below the stipulated limit. But now their avarice got the better of their forbearance, and they called loudly for the immediate division of the gold. To wait longer would only be to invite the assault of their enemies, allured by a bait so attractive. While the treasure remained uncounted, no man knew its value, nor what was to be his own portion. It was better to distribute it at once, and let every one possess and defend his own. Several, moreover, were now disposed to return home and take their share of the gold with them, where they could place it in safety. But these were few; while much the larger part were only anxious to leave their present quarters and march at once to Cuzco. More gold, they thought, awaited them in that capital than they could get here by prolonging their stay; while every hour was precious, to prevent the inhabitants from secreting their treasures, of which design they had already given indication.

Pizarro was especially moved by the last consideration; and he felt that without the capital he could not hope to become master of the empire. Without further delay, the division of the treasure was agreed upon.

Gold and Gold-Hunters

Yet, before making this, it was necessary to reduce the whole to ingots of a uniform standard, for the spoil was composed of an infinite variety of articles, in which the gold was of very different degrees of purity. These articles consisted of goblets, ewers, salvers, vases of every shape and size, ornaments and utensils for the temples of the royal palaces, tiles and plates for the decoration of the public edifices, curious imitations of different plants and animals. Among the plants, the most beautiful was the Indian corn, in which the golden ear was sheathed in its broad leaves of silver, from which hung a rich tassel of threads of the same precious metal. A fountain was also much admired, which sent up a sparkling jet of gold, while birds and animals of the same material played in the waters at its base. The delicacy of the workmanship of some of these, and the beauty and ingenuity of the design, attracted the admiration of better judges than the rude Conquerors of Peru ...

The division of the ransom being completed by the Spaniards, there seemed to be no further obstacle to their resuming active operations and commencing the march to Cuzco. But what was to be done with Atahualpa? In the determination of this question, whatever was expedient was just. To liberate him would be to set at large the very man who might prove their most dangerous enemy – one whose birth and royal station would rally round him the whole nation, place all the machinery of government at his control, and all its resources – one, in short, whose bare word might concentrate all the energies of his people against the Spaniards, and thus delay for a long period, if not wholly defeat, the conquest of the country. Yet to hold him in captivity was attended with scarcely less difficulty, since to guard so important a prize would require such a division of their force as must greatly cripple its strength, and how could they expect, by any vigilance, to secure their prisoner against rescue in the perilous passes of the mountains?

The Inca himself now loudly demanded his freedom. The proposed amount of the ransom had, indeed, not been fully paid. It may be doubted whether it ever would have been, considering the embarrassments thrown in the way by the guardians of the temples, who seemed disposed to secrete the treasures rather than despoil these sacred depositories to satisfy the cupidity of the strangers. It was unlucky, too, for the Indian monarch that much of the gold, and that of the best quality, consisted of flat plates or tiles, which, however valuable, lay in compact form that did little towards swelling the heap. But an immense amount had been already realized, and it would have been a still greater one, the Inca might allege, but for the impatience of the Spaniards. At all events, it was a magnificent ransom, such as was never paid by prince or potentate before.

The solution to the problem of Atahualpa's future was tragically simple. He was brought to trial and accused of usurping his crown, inciting his people to rebellion against the conquerors, and of practising idolatry and polygamy. Atahualpa was found guilty and sentenced to be burned alive. Prescott takes up the story again:

When the sentence was communicated to the Inca, he was greatly overcome by it. He had, indeed, for some time, looked to such an issue as probable, and had been heard to intimate as much to those about him ... For a moment, the overwhelming conviction of it unmanned him, and he exclaimed, with tears in his eyes, 'What have I done, or my children, that I should meet such a fate? And from your hands, too,' said he, addressing Pizarro; 'you, who have met with friendship and kindness from my people, with whom I have shared my treasures, who have received nothing but benefits from my hands!' In the most piteous tones, he then implored that his life might be spared. promising any guarantee

Left: *Peruvian gold beaker in the National Museum of Archaeology, Lima*
Above: *an Inca silver dish and gold beaker in the British Museum*
Below left: *a Peruvian gold 'whistling vase' now at Dumbarton Oaks, Washington*
Below: *a Chimu god of gold and turquoise – the handle of a ceremonial knife*

that might be required for the safety of every Spaniard in the army – promising double the ransom he had already paid, if time were only given to obtain it.

An eye-witness assures us that Pizarro was visibly affected as he turned away from the Inca, to whose appeal he had no power to listen in opposition to the voice of the army and to his own sense of what was due to the security of the country. Atahualpa, finding he had no power to turn his Conqueror from his purpose, recovered his habitual self-possession, and from that moment submitted himself to his fate with the courage of an Indian warrior.

But the story was not quite ended. Atahualpa was now told that if he consented to become a Christian and be baptized, the punishment would be commuted to mere strangulation by the garrotte. Atahualpa agreed.

With the death of Atahualpa, Pizarro had achieved all the power and all the gold. All the gold? Not quite. The rest of Atahualpa's ransom was never found and, all over Peru, Inca priests hastily buried their golden treasures before they could be appropriated by the Spanish invaders. Today, four hundred years after the death of the last Inca, the search for his gold still goes on.

The search for El Dorado

The Spanish were not content with the acquisition of the golden treasures of Mexico and Peru. Surely, among the dense jungles of central and south America, other civilizations were waiting to be pillaged? Surely there were further golden cities to be sacked, new treasures to be found? Soon rumours spread of a fabulous golden city, standing near a lake, which offered wealth and riches far in excess of those previously found. This legendary city, known as El Dorado, had developed from stories which the Spaniards had heard about the existence of *El hombre dorado*, the gilded man – a king who, in some sort of ritual observance, covered himself in gold dust before bathing in a lake. The legend varied. According to one version the king spent his days covered in gold dust which he washed away each night in order to sleep in comfort. In another, the ceremonial immersion took place in a lake where the wife of an earlier king had drowned herself. The immersion only took place on the accession of each new king, who plunged into the lake, covered in gold dust, as a form of symbolic sacrifice. But, though the legend may have varied, people continued to believe in the existence of the fabulous golden city and many expeditions set out to find it. All failed, and El Dorado remains a tantalizing myth, a symbol of legendary wealth.

The gilded man, though, no doubt existed in one form or another, and the lake where his ritual ducking took place has been identified as Lake Guatavita in Colombia. Alexander von Humboldt, the celebrated German naturalist, visited the lake at the beginning of the nineteenth century and saw on its banks a staircase cut into the rock for ablution ceremonies. He saw, too, the evidence of early Spanish attempts to drain the lake and recover the treasure which they felt sure was buried in its depths. In 1903 a British excavation attempt was defeated by the depth of silt at the bottom of the lake.

But, by that time, new sources of gold had been discovered, not in spectacular cities or mythical lakes, but in the rocks and rivers of California and the Klondike, the Transvaal and New South Wales.

5. The great gold rushes

'Some kind of mettle that looks like goald'

On Monday 24 January 1848, a young Mormon workman at a sawmill on the American River in California wrote in his diary:

> This day some kind of mettle was found in the tail race that looks like goald, first discovered by James Martial, the Boss of the Mill.

The 'mettle' was indeed gold, but the writer of those few clumsily spelled words could not have foreseen that the discovery would have far-reaching effects on the isolated valleys of California, and that it would change the course of history in his own country and elsewhere.

The discovery was quite accidental. James Marshall arrived in California in 1845. He found work there with John A. Sutter, a prosperous Swiss landowner, who employed him to build and operate a sawmill on the American River. Marshall himself told the story of what happened next in an article published in the *Century Illustrated Monthly Magazine* in 1891:

> One morning in January, it was a clear cold morning; I shall never forget that morning, as I was taking my usual walk along the race, after shutting off the water, my eye was caught by a glimpse of something shining in the bottom of the ditch. There was about a foot of water running there. I reached my hand down and picked it up; it made my heart thump for I felt certain it was gold. The piece was about half the size and of the shape of a pea. Then I saw another piece in the water. After taking it out, I sat down and began to think right hard. I thought it was gold, and yet it did not seem to be of the right colour; all the gold coin I had seen was of a reddish tinge; this looked more like brass. I recalled to mind all the metals I had ever seen or heard of, but I could find none that resembled this. Suddenly the idea flashed across my mind that it might be iron pyrites. I trembled to think of it! This question could soon be determined. Putting one of the pieces on hard river stone, I took another and commenced hammering it. It was soft and didn't

A facsimile of the entry in Bigler's diary recording the discovery of gold by James Marshall at Sutter's Mill, 24 January 1848

James Marshall

and John A. Sutter

break; it therefore must be gold, but largely mixed with some other metal, very likely silver; for pure gold, I thought, would certainly have a brighter colour.

When I returned to our cabin for breakfast I showed the two pieces to my men. They were all a good deal excited, and had they not thought that the gold only existed in small quantities they would have abandoned everything and left me to finish the job alone. However, to satisfy them, I told them that as soon as we had the mill finished we would devote a week or two to gold hunting and see what we could make out of it.

While we were working in the race after this discovery, we always kept a sharp lookout, and in the course of three or four days we had picked up about three ounces – our work still progressing as lively as ever, for none of us imagined at the time that the whole country was sowed with gold.

About a week's time after the discovery I had to take another trip to the fort; and to gain what information I could respecting the real value of the metal, took all we had collected with me and showed it to Mr Sutter, who at once declared it was gold, but thought with me, it was greatly mixed with some other metal. It puzzled us a great deal to hit upon the means of telling the exact quantity contained in the alloy; however, we at last stumbled on an old American cyclopedia where we saw the specific gravity of all the metals, and rules given to find the quantity of each in a given bulk. After hunting over the whole fort and borrowing from some of the men, we got three dollars and a half in silver, and with a small pair of scales we soon cyphered it out that there was no silver nor copper in the gold, but that it was entirely pure.

This fact being ascertained, we thought it our best policy to keep it as quiet as possible till we should have finished our mill, but there was a great number of disbanded Mormon soldiers in and about the fort, and when they came to hear of it, why, it just spread like wildfire, and soon the whole country was in a bustle. I had scarcely arrived at the mill again till several persons appeared with pans, shovels, and hoes, and those that had not iron picks had wooden ones, all anxious to fall to work and dig up our mill; but this we would not permit. As fast as one party disappeared another would arrive, and sometimes I had the greatest kind of trouble to get rid of them. I sent them all off in different directions, telling them about such and such places, where I was certain there was plenty of gold if they would only take the trouble of looking for it. At that time I never imagined the gold was so abundant. I told them to go to such and such places, because it appeared that they would dig nowhere but in such places as I pointed out, and I believe such was their confidence in me that they would have dug on the very top of yon mountain if I had told them to do so ...

So there, stranger, is the entire history of the gold discovery in California – a discovery that hasn't as yet been of much benefit to me.

Marshall's momentous discovery was to bring him no benefit at all. He had no share in the riches that were unearthed around him when the news of the finds leaked out. Miners attacked him in their desperation to find gold. He was accused of deliberately concealing the existence of rich lodes and his life was threatened more than once by drunken mobs of diggers. He died in abject poverty in 1885, having lived to see California transformed by the events which followed his discovery.

The California Trail

It was Sam Brannan, a storekeeper at Sutter's Fort, who brought the news of James Marshall's discovery to San Francisco in May 1848. It is said that he rode through the streets waving a bottle of gold dust and shouting, 'Gold! Gold! Gold! Gold from the American River!'

An immediate stampede to the diggings began. Workmen downed tools, doctors and lawyers left their offices, tradesmen deserted their stores. Children were left without teachers. Hotels and newspapers were forced to close down. Within a month

Where the gold was found – Sutter's Mill on the American River, Coloma, California

CAU

three-quarters of the houses in San Francisco were standing empty.

The news spread like wildfire to other Californian settlements but it was only at the end of the year, when President Polk gave official confirmation of the rumours that had already seeped eastwards, that the storm broke, and thousands of gold hunters set out on the perilous journey to California. 'The accounts of the abundance of gold are of such an extraordinary character as would scarcely command belief,' the President told Congress in December, 'were they not corroborated by the authentic reports of officers in the public service.'

The President's words convinced those who had not been impressed by less reliable informants. Newspapers sang the praises of California and the wealth that its gold could offer. Over fifty thousand Americans were infected by the fever and set out for the diggings. The infection spread to other countries and it is estimated that, all told, over eighty thousand people made the journey to California. Gold fever spread into all aspects of American life. The shops were suddenly filled with the clothing and equipment needed for a mining expedition. Books were hastily published to offer emigrants advice on mining methods and the best routes to the diggings. Complex and improbable mining machinery was swiftly developed for sale to the intending prospector. Thus equipped and encumbered, the forty-niners set out to

Gold and Gold-Hunters

With the discovery of gold in California 'gold fever' hit America and people in many other countries. The forty-niners, as they came to be called, travelled to California, suffering tremendous hardship on the way. This picture shows the forty-niners sailing round Cape Horn to California

seek their fortunes, many of them probably singing one of the popular variations of 'Oh Susanna':

> I come from Salem City
>   With my washbowl on my knee,
> I'm going to California
>   This gold dust for to see.
> It rained all night the day I left,
>   The weather it was dry,
> The sun so hot I froze to death,
>   Oh, brothers, don't you cry!
>
> Oh, California,
>   That's the land for me.
> I'm bound for San Francisco
>   With my washbowl on my knee.

There were three principal routes to California. All were perilous and many hopeful forty-niners did not survive the journey. The safest route was by sea round Cape Horn; the shortest route took the traveller by ship to Panama and then across the isthmus to the Pacific coast. The most popular route, though, was overland. In 1849 thousands of forty-niners set out from the Missouri River along the trails that led westward to California. Many of them died on the five-month journey, and all of them faced hardship and danger.

Some of the emigrants have left diaries of their journeys. Among these was J. Goldsborough Bruff, whose journal and drawings give a vivid and authentic picture of the hardships endured by the travellers:

July 8, 1849... At 1 p.m. poor Bishop died, of Cholera. The first casualty in the Company, sudden and astounding, was this very mysterious and fatal visitation. Yesterday, in presence of the deceased, I remarked how very fortunate we had been, in all respects, and trusted we might continue so. The messmates of the deceased laid him out, sewed him up in his blue blanket, and prepared a bier, formed of his tent-poles. I had a grave dug in a neighboring ridge, on the left of the trail, about 400 yards from it. Dry clay and gravel, and coarse white sand-stone on the next hill afforded slabs to line it with, making a perfect vault. I sat 3 hours in the hot sun, and sculptured a head and foot stone; and filled the letters with blacking from the hub of a wheel.

I then organized a funeral procession, men all in clean clothes and uniforms, with music (a key-bugle, flute, violin and accordion) and two and two, with Stars & stripes over the body, we marched to the measured time of the dirge, deposited the body of our comrade in the grave, an elderly gentleman read the burial service, and we filled up the grave, erected the stones, and returned to camp.

Oct. 31st, 1849 About 1 o'clock this morning we were awakened by a man, crying at the top of his voice, '*Hallo, here! Turn out and assist, a tree has fallen on a couple of tents, and killed and wounded several persons!*' We promptly turned out, in the rain, lit a lantern, aroused our friends, and proceeded to the fatal spot. About 100 yds. in rear of my tent, a large oak tree, decayed near the ground, became heavy with the moisture, and probably a gust of wind assisted, and it fell, partially over a tent close to its base, and directly across another tent, 20 paces further, in which lay 4 men, side by side. A large limb, capable of making a couple of cords of fuel, had to be cut off, and then the long heavy trunk pryed with levers and rolled off, consequently mutilating the lower extremities of the unfortunate wretches beneath it. Then we raised the blood-stained tent, cut it off from the chords, and extricated the broken tent-poles, &c. and there lay a shocking sight! An aged, grey headed man, and his grown son, with their hips buried in the ground, and their ghastly eyes turned up in death! Next another son, and beside him, a young man, his comrade, slowly dying in agony, with broken legs and mutilated bodies – groaning, and uttering the name of God, in acute suffering! The screaming of the females, the grey-headed mother kissing their pallid brows while her silver hairs swept their faces, and then she would groan & scream – and her 2 grown daughters stood, with clasped hands, choking sobs, and eyes upraised to Heaven, regardless of the bleak storm and rain. While the few men, to succor them, were moving around with lanterns. Whilst extricating the tent from over these unfortunate men, some attended to the tent at the foot of the tree; it was soon cleared away, while a little girl within was crying, saying her stomach was hurt, and another that her feet were hurt. These two were slightly bruised and sprained, while several other little children with them escaped any injury. A large limb of the tree had first struck the ground, twisting the lower end of the tree over, so as merely to knock over the tent, & slightly hurt the children; while the same cause projected the body of the tree across the tent of the men. The old man and one son died in half an hour after the accident ... Busy with the dead & dying all day. At dusk we chopped wood, and built up a good fire for these unhappy people. About 1 hour after dark, the 2nd son died. Willis and Grissom sat up with them. They said it was a shocking sight to witness. The dying son turning his head in agony – on one side saw his dead brother, and on the other his dying friend. The young man died about day-break.

Tragedy was to come to Bruff too. When winter overtook his party, he volunteered to stay with the snowbound wagons while his companions pressed on to get help. Despite their promises, none of them returned to his aid. Ill and alone, Bruff faced the prospect of slow starvation.

J. Goldsborough Bruff is one of the forty-niners who left a journal and pictures of the overland trek to California. They tell their own tale of the perils they had to survive:

A capsized wagon, June 1849

Crossing the River Platte, July 1849

The Bruff wagon train camping along the Sweetwater River, Wyoming
    By the autumn of 1849 some of the emigrants were wagonless and travelling on foot

April 1st, 1850 Hail lies thick on the ground. About daybreak I left the cabin, and went to my tent to lie down, but was too cold to sleep much. I lay, hoping for repose, till sun-rise, when I built up my fire, made coffee, and warmed a pint of the bone-tea; but attending to the coffee, my kettle of broth fell over, and I thus lost my *last meal*! I picked up the pieces of bone & gnawed them, drank my coffee, and ate a spoonful of the grounds ...

General debility, and rheumatism in back and calves of legs, have hobbled me. Yet I must exert myself, or die at once; and they say that 'whilst there's life, there's Hope.' Indeed there is! ...

I shouldered my carbine, put cartridges in my pouch, and started; I proceeded about 2 miles, on the road, and then gave out. I saw 2 deer across a ravine, and numerous wild-pidgeons, grouse, woodpeckers, robins, crows, &c. But fate had marked me; they knew it, and kept beyond my reach. After a lethargic rest, I retraced my painful steps, reached my lone shelter, and threw me, again exhausted, on my damp pallet. On recovering, the keen cravings of hunger warned me of the imperious necessity to procure food immediately. I recollected that Roberts had put a deer's head under the eaves of the cabin, a long time since, where it became wedged in the logs, and he could not conveniently extricate it, to give to the dogs. This I sought. Ha! I have food! I thought. On reaching it, I with much difficulty got it down by the aid of a pole; and found it half decayed, and consumed by worms & insects. However, I took it to a stump near my tent, chopped it up with a hatchet, and cut out the shrivelled tongue ... Put the small half of the tongue in a kettle to cook. While this was boiling, I overhauled the skins again, and found one, of a fawn, with the hoofs and fetlock-joints attached. These I cut off, scraped out the worms, singed off most of the hair, and threw them also in the kettle. Then I made coffee, and thank God! had another meal with some solid food; which possessed a queer taste; and would have been, probably, in different circumstances, quite disgusting!

Bruff survived his ordeal and arrived, at last, at the diggings. But, like many of those who took the California Trail, he failed to make his fortune.

Rocking the cradle

Life at the diggings was hard and monotonous. Few of the new arrivals knew anything about mining, and many were surprised to discover that gold had to be *dug* from the ground and wasn't lying on the surface, waiting to be picked up. Although rich strikes were made and fortunes won for some, most of the forty-niners could only scrape a meagre living from their claims.

The journal of Daniel Woods, a Philadelphia schoolteacher who travelled to California in 1849, paints a sobering picture of the hardships which the diggers experienced, as well as a fascinating account of the methods which they used to find gold:

Salmon Falls, South Fork of the American River – July 4

Here we are, at length, in the gold diggings. Seated around us, upon the ground, beneath a large oak, are a group of wild Indians, from the tribe called 'Diggers'. They have brought us in some salmon, one of which weighs 29 pounds. These they spear with great dexterity, and exchange for provisions, or clothing, and ornaments of bright colours.

We are surrounded on all sides by high, steep mountains, over which are scattered the evergreen and white oak, and which are inhabited by the wolf and the bear. We have spent the day in 'prospecting', a term which designates a very important part of the business of mining. In order to find the gold the ground must be prospected. A spot is first selected, in the choice of which science has little and chance everything to do. The stones and loose upper soil, as also the subsoil, almost down to the primitive rock, are removed. Upon or near this rock most of the gold is found, and it is the object in every mining operation, to reach this rock, however great the labor, even though it lies forty, eighty or one hundred feet beneath the surface. If, when this strata rock is attained, it is found to present a smooth surface, it may as well be abandoned at once; if seamed with crevices, running at angles with the river, the prospect of the miner is favorable. Some of the dirt is then put into a pan, taken to the water and washed out with great care. The miner stoops down by the stream and dipping a quantity of water into the pan with the dirt, stirs it about with his hands, washing and throwing out the large pebbles, till the dirt is thoroughly wet. More water is then taken into the pan, the whole mass well stirred and shaken,

Forty-Niner's Slang

Most close-knit communities develop their own jargon or slang and the miners in the California gold rush were no exception. Many of the words they used derived from Spanish, for California was ruled by Mexico until 1848. Here are some examples from the miners' colourful vocabulary:

Ripsniptious: smart or tidy
Have the peedoodles: to be nervous or excited
Conbobberation: a row or a fuss
Chispa or *spark:* a tiny piece of gold
Quicks: fleas
Slows: lice
Bonanza: a very rich vein of gold; a stroke of good fortune
Borrasca: the opposite of 'bonanza'
Seeing the elephant: the 'elephant' was a symbol of the lure of gold and all the excitement, hardship and disappointments that accompanied the search for it. The phrase is said to originate in an old story about a farmer whose cart of produce was overturned when a circus came to the market. 'I don't give a hang,' he said. 'I have seen the elephant.'

Thy travels are over...

Many gold-hunters died on the long and perilous journey to California. J. Goldsborough Bruff noted these grave inscriptions as he followed the California Trail westwards:

LEMUEL LEE,
OF VANDALIA, ILL :-
DIED JUNE 3, 1849,
AT 4 P.M. AGED
64 YEARS: DIED OF
PROSTRATION CONSEQUENT
UPON CHOLERA AFTER AN
ILLNESS OF 2 WEEKS.

AN INDIAN SQUAW;
JUNE 27TH. 1849,
KILL'D BY A FALL FROM
A HORSE, NEAR THIS PLACE:
CALM BE HER SLEEP, AND SWEET
HER REST.
BE KIND TO THE INDIAN.

JNO. A. DAWSON,
ST. LOUIS, MO.
DIED OCT. 1st 1849,
FROM EATING A POISONOUS
ROOT AT THE SPRING.

FRANCIS PICKERING,
OF VICINITY OF BOSTON,
MASS:
AGED 35 YEARS.
SHOT BY INDIANS, 90
MILES E. OF THIS,
AUG: 25. 1850.
RESPECTED & ESTEEMED
BY
ALL WHO KNEW HIM.

JNO. CAMPBELL,
OF LAFAYETTE CO. MO.
CAME TO HIS DEATH BY THE
ACCIDENTAL DISCHARGE
OF HIS GUN, WHILE RIDING
WITH A FRIEND, JUNE 21.
1849. AGED 18 YEARS.

JNO HOOVER, DIED, JUNE 18. 49
AGED 12 YRS. REST IN PEACE,
SWEET BOY.
FOR THY TRAVELS ARE OVER.

ROBERT GILMORE
AND WIFE,
DIED OF CHOLERA,
JULY 18TH. 1849.

ALLEN McLANE,
OCTr 9TH. 1849,
PLATTE CO. MO. AGED 36 YRS:-
DISEASE GASTRO ENTERITES
TYPHOID.

and the top gravel thrown off with the fingers while the gold, being heavier, sinks deeper into the pan. It is then shaken about, more water being continually added, and thrown off with a sideway motion which carries with it the dirt at the top, while the gold settles yet lower down. When the dirt is nearly washed out great care is requisite to prevent the lighter scales of gold from being washed out with the sand. At length a ridge of gold scales, mixed with a little sand, remains in the pan, from the quantity of which some estimate may be formed of the richness of the place. If there are five to eight grains it is considered that it will pay. If less, the miner digs deeper or opens a new hole, until he finds a place affording a good prospect. When this is done he sets his cradle by the side of the stream and proceeds to wash all the dirt. Thus have we been employed the whole of this day, digging one hole after another, washing out many test pans, hoping at every new attempt to find that which would reward our toil – and we have made ten cents each.

July 6th
We have today removed to the opposite side of the river. This, with pitching our tent, has occupied most of the day. Still, we made $4 each. For several hours I have been seated by the river side rocking a heavy cradle filled with dirt and stones. The working of a cradle requires from three to five persons, according to the character of the diggings. If there is much of the auriferous dirt and it is easily obtained, three are sufficient; but if there is little soil and this found in crevices, so as to be obtained only by digging out with a knife, five or more can be employed in keeping the cradle in operation. One of these gives his whole attention to working the cradle, another takes the dirt to be washed, in pans or buckets, from the hole to the cradle, while one or more others fill the buckets.

The cradle, so called from its general resemblance to that article of furniture, is placed at the edge of the water so that the person rocking it may at the same time dip up water. The dirt is gradually washed out, the mud being carried off in the stream. Cleats are nailed across the bottom of the cradle, over which the loose dirt passes with the water and behind which the gold settles. Twenty-five buckets of dirt are usually washed through, the residue being then drawn off through holes at the bottom of the cradle, and 'panned' out or washed in the same manner as in prospecting. While this is being done by one of the company, the others commonly spend the ten minutes' interval in resting themselves. Seated

Prospectors at work panning and using rockers and cradles

upon the rocks about their companion they watch the ridge of gold as it dimples brightly up amid the black sand. At length, the washing completed, the pan passes from one to another, while each one gives his opinion as to the quantity. The holes in the bottom of the cradle are then stopped up, more dirt is thrown into the hopper and again the grating, scraping sounds are heard which are peculiar to the rocking of the cradle – which, years hence, will accompany our dreams of the mines.

July 10th
We made $3 each today. This life of hardships and exposure has affected my health. Our diet consists of hard tack, flour we eat half cooked, and salt pork, with occasionally a salmon which we purchase from the Indians. Vegetables are not to be procured. Our feet are wet all day, while a hot sun shines down upon our heads and the very air parches the skin like the hot air of an oven. Our drinking water comes down to us thoroughly impregnated with the mineral substances washed through the thousand cradles above us. After our days of labor, exhausted and faint, we retire – if this word may be applied to the simple act of lying down in our clothes – robbing our feet of their boots to make a pillow of them, and wrapping our blankets about us, on a bed of pine boughs, or on the ground beneath

the clear, bright stars of the night. Near morning there is always a change in the temperature and several blankets become necessary. The feet and the hands of a novice in this business become blistered and lame, and the limbs are stiff. Besides all these causes of sickness, the anxieties and cares which wear away the lives of so many men who leave their families to come to this land of gold, contribute, in no small degree, to the same result.

All that glitters . . .

The discovery of gold transformed California from an isolated pastoral community into a vigorous and prosperous territory with, in 1852, a population of over a quarter of a million people. When the gold yield began to decline in the 1850s, the miners were only too willing to try their luck elsewhere. Rich finds on the Fraser River in British Columbia drew many diggers northwards but most of them flocked to Nevada in the first years of the 1860s when the legendary Comstock Lode of silver and gold was discovered near Virginia City.

Among the thousands who flocked to Nevada was Mark Twain, famous now for his books *Tom Sawyer* and *Huckleberry Finn*, but then a young reporter on the local newspaper. In his autobiographical book, *Roughing It*, Twain recalled his life in the vigorous mining community of Virginia City and, in one entertaining episode, his own attempt at prospecting:

I confess, without shame, that I expected to find masses of silver lying all about the ground. I expected to see it glittering in the sun on the mountain summits. I said nothing about this, for some instinct told me that I might possibly have

Break for a photograph?
Four forty-niners

THE MINERS' TEN COMMANDMENTS.

A man spake these words, and said: I am a miner, who wandered "from a way down east, and came to sojourn in a strange land, and 'see the elephant.'" And behold I saw him, and bear witness, that from the key of his trunk to the end of his tail, his whole body has passed before me; and I followed him until his huge feet stood still before a clapboard shanty; then with his trunk extended, he pointed to a candle card tacked upon a shingle, as though he would say Read, and I read the

MINERS' TEN COMMANDMENTS.

I.

Thou shalt have no other claim than one.

II.

Thou shalt not make unto thyself any false claim, nor any likeness to a mean man, by jumping one; whatever thou findest on the top above or on the rock beneath, or in a crevice underneath the rock;—or I will visit the miners around to invite them on my side; and when they decide against thee, thou shalt take thy pick and thy pan, thy shovel and thy blankets, with all that thou hast, and "go prospecting" to seek good diggings; but thou shalt find none. Then, when thou hast returned, in sorrow shalt thou find that thine old claim is worked out, and yet no pile made thee to hide in the ground, or in an old boot beneath thy bunk, or in buckskin or bottle underneath thy cabin; but hast paid all that was in thy purse away, worn out thy boots and thy garments, so that there is nothing good about them but the pockets, and thy patience is likened unto thy garments; and at last thou shalt hire thy body out to make thy board and save thy bacon.

III.

Thou shalt go prospecting before thy claim gives out. Neither shalt thou take thy money, nor thy gold dust, nor thy good name, to the gaming table in vain; for monte, twenty-one, roulette, faro, lansquenet and poker, will prove to thee that thou more thou puttest down the less thou shalt take up; and when thou thinkest of thy wife and children, thou shalt not hold thyself guiltless—but in sane.

IV.

Thou shalt not remember what thy friends do at home on the Sabbath day, lest the remembrance may not compare favorably with what thou doest here.—Six days thou mayest dig or pick all that thy body can stand under; but the other day is Sunday; yea thou washest all thy dirty shirts, darnest all thy stockings, tap thy boots, mend thy clothing, chop thy whole week's firewood, make up and bake thy bread, and boil thy pork and beans, that thou wait not when thou returnest from thy long-tom weary. For in six days' labor only thou canst not work enough to wear out thy body in two years; but if thou workest hard on Sunday also, thou canst do it in six months; and thou, and thy son, and thy daughter, thy male friend and thy female friend, thy morals and thy conscience, be none the better for it; but reproach thee, shouldst thou ever return with thy worn-out body to thy mother's fireside; and thou shalt not strive to justify thyself, because the trader and the blacksmith, the carpenter and the merchant, the tailors, Jews, and buccaneers, defy God and civilization, by keeping not the Sabbath day, nor wish for a day of rest, such as memory, youth and home, made hallowed.

V.

Thou shalt not think more of all thy gold, and how thou canst make it fastest, than how thou wilt enjoy it, after thou hast ridden rough-shod over thy good old parents' precepts and examples, that thou mayest have nothing to reproach and sting thee, when thou art left alone in the log where thy father's blessing and thy mother's love hath sent thee.

VI.

Thou shalt not kill thy body by working in the rain, even though thou shalt make enough to buy physic and attendance with. Neither shalt thou kill thy neighbor's body in a duel; for by "keeping cool," thou canst save his life and thy conscience. Neither shalt thou destroy thyself by getting "tight," nor "slewed," nor "high," nor "corned," nor "half-seas over," nor "three sheets in the wind," by drinking smoothly down—"brandy slings," "gin cocktails," "whisky punches," "rum toddies," nor "egg nogs." Neither shalt thou suck "mint-juleps," nor "sherry-cobblers," through a straw, nor gurgle from a bottle the "raw material," nor "take it neat" from a decanter; for, while thou art wallowing down thy purse, and thy coat from off thy back, thou art burning the coat from off thy stomach; and, if thou couldst see the homes and lands, and gold dust, and home comforts already lying there—"a huge pile"—thou shouldst feel a choking in thy throat; and when to that thou addest thy crooked walkings and hiccupping talkings, of lodgings in the gutter, of drowlings in the sun, of prospect-holes half full of water, and of shafts and ditches, from which thou hast emerged like a drowning rat, thou wilt feel disgusted with thyself, and inquire, "Is thy servant a dog that he doeth these things?" verily I will say, Farewell, old bottle, I will kiss thy gurgling lips no more. And thou, slings, cocktails, punches, smashes, cobblers, nogs, toddies, sangarees, and juleps, forever farewell. Thy remembrance shames me; henceforth, "I cut thy acquaintance," and headaches, tremblings, heart burnings, blue devils, and all the indirect causing-up of evils that follow in thy train. My wife's smiles and my children's merry-hearted laugh, shall charm and reward me for having the manly firmness and courage to say No. I wish thee an eternal farewell.

VII.

Thou shalt not grow discouraged, nor think of going home before thou hast made thy "pile," because thou hast not "struck a lead," nor found a "rich crevice," nor sunk a hole upon a "pocket," lest in going home thou shalt leave four dollars a day, and go to work, ashamed, at fifty cents, and serve thee right; for thou knowest by staying here, thou mightst strike a lead and of y dollars a day, and keep thy manly self-respect, and then go home with enough to make thyself and others happy.

VIII.

Thou shalt not steal a pick, or a shovel, or a pan from thy fellow miner; nor take away his tools without his leave; nor borrow those he cannot spare; nor return them broken, nor trouble him to fetch them back again, nor talk with him while his water rent is running on, nor remove his stake to enlarge thy claim, nor undermine his bank in following a lead, nor pan out gold from his "riffle box," nor wash the "tailings" from his sluice's mouth. Neither shalt thou pick out specimens from the company's pan to put them in thy mouth, or in thy purse; nor cheat thy partner of his share; nor steal from thy cabin mate his gold dust, to add to thine, for he will be sure to discover what thou hast done, and will straightway call his fellow miners together, and if the law hinder them not, they will hang thee, or give thee fifty lashes, or shave thy head and brand thee, like a horse thief, with "R" upon thy cheek, to be known and read of all men, Californians in particular.

IX.

Thou shalt not tell any false tales about "good diggings in the mountains," to thy neighbor, that thou mayest benefit a friend who hath mules, and provisions, and tools and blankets, he cannot sell,—lest in deceiving thy neighbor, when he returneth through the snow with nought save his rifle, he present thee with the contents thereof, and like a dog, thou shalt fall down and die.

X.

Thou shalt not commit unsuitable matrimony, nor covet "single blessedness;" nor forget absent maidens; nor neglect thy "first love,"—but thou shalt consider how faithfully and patiently she waiteth thy return; yea, and covereth each epistle that thou sendest with kisses of kindly welcome—until she hath thyself. Neither shalt thou covet thy neighbor's wife, nor trifle with the affections of his daughter; yet, if thy heart be free, and thou dost love and covet each other, thou shalt "pop the question" like a man, lest mother, more manly than thou art, should step in before thee, and thou love her in vain, and in the anguish of thy heart's disappointment, thou shalt quote the language of the great, and say, "such is life," and thy future lot be that of a poor, lonely, deserted and comfortless bachelor.

A new Commandment give I unto thee —if thou hast a wife and little ones, that thou lovest dearer than thy life,—that thou keep them continually before thee, to cheer and urge thee onward until thou canst say, "I have enough—God bless them—I will return." Then as thou journiest towards thy much loved home, with open arms shall they come forth to welcome thee, and falling upon thy neck with tears of unutterable joy that thou art come; then in the fullness of thy heart's gratitude, thou shalt kneel together before thy Heavenly Father, to thank Him for thy safe return. AMEN —So mote it be.

FORTY-NINE.

an exaggerated idea about it, and so if I betrayed my thought I might bring derision upon myself. Yet I was as perfectly satisfied in my own mind, as I could be of anything, that I was going to gather up, in a day or two, or at furthest a week or two, silver enough to make me satisfactorily wealthy – and so my fancy was already busy with plans for spending this money. The first opportunity that offered, I sauntered carelessly away from the cabin, keeping an eye on the other boys, and stopping and contemplating the sky when they seemed to be observing me; but as soon as the coast was manifestly clear, I fled away as guiltily as a thief might have done and never halted till I was far beyond sight and call. Then I began my search with a feverish excitement that was brimful of expectation – almost of certainty. I crawled about the ground, seizing and examining bits of stone, blowing the dust from them or rubbing them on my clothes, and then peering at them with anxious hope. Presently I found a bright fragment and my heart bounded! I hid behind a boulder and polished it and scrutinized it with a nervous eagerness and a delight that was more pronounced than absolute certainty itself could have afforded. The more I examined the fragment, the more I was convinced that I had found the door to fortune. I marked the spot and carried away my specimen. Up and down the rugged mountain-side I searched, with always increasing interest and always augmenting gratitude that I had come to Humboldt County and come in time. Of all the experiences of my life, this secret search among the hidden treasures of silver land was the

Samuel Langhorne Clemens – or Mark Twain – who spent some time prospecting for gold

Left: *J. M. Hutchings was one of many forty-niners who were unlucky in the California diggings, but he was to make his fortune in a different way. In 1853 he wrote and printed a broadsheet called* The Miners' Ten Commandments *which was so popular that he was able to retire from mining on the proceeds of the 100,000 copies which he sold*

nearest to unmarred ecstasy. It was a delirious revel. By and by, in the bed of a shallow rivulet, I found a deposit of shining yellow scales, and my breath almost forsook me! A gold mine, and in my simplicity I had been content with vulgar silver! I was so excited that I half believed my overwrought imagination was deceiving me. Then a fear came upon me that people might be observing me and would guess my secret. Moved by this thought, I made a circuit of the place, and ascended a knoll to reconnoitre. Solitude. No creature was near. Then I returned to my

A mining camp

mine, fortifying myself against possible disappointment, but my fears were groundless – the shining scales were still there. I set about scooping them out, and for an hour I toiled down the windings of the stream and robbed its bed. But at last the descending sun warned me to give up the quest, and I turned homeward laden with wealth. As I walked along I could not help smiling at the thought of my being so excited over my fragment of silver when a nobler metal was almost under my nose. In this little time the former had so fallen in my estimation that once or twice I was on the point of throwing it away.

The boys were as hungry as usual, but I could eat nothing. Neither could I talk. I was full of dreams and far away. Their conversation interrupted the flow of my fancy somewhat, and annoyed me a little, too. I despised the sordid and commonplace things they talked about. But as they proceeded, it began to amuse me. It grew to be rare fun to hear them planning their poor little economies and sighing over possible privations and distresses when a gold mine, all our own, lay within sight of the cabin and I could point it out at any moment. Smothered hilarity began to oppress me, presently. It was hard to resist the impulse to burst out with exultation and reveal everything; but I did resist. I said within myself that I would filter the great news through my lips calmly and be serene as a summer morning while I watched its effect in their faces. I said:

'Where have you all been?'

'Prospecting.'

'What did you find?'

'Nothing.'

'Nothing? What do you think of the country?'

'Can't tell, yet,' said Mr Ballou, who was an old gold miner, and had likewise had considerable experience among the silver mines.

'Well, haven't you formed any sort of opinion?'

'Yes, a sort of a one. It's fair enough here, maybe, but overrated. Seven-thousand-dollar ledges are scarce, though. That Sheba may be rich enough, but we don't own it; and besides, the rock is so full of base metals that all the science in the world can't work it. We'll not starve here, but we'll not get rich, I'm afraid.'

'So you think the prospect is pretty poor?'

'No name for it!'

'Well, we'd better go back, hadn't we?'

'Oh, not yet – of course not. We'll try it a riffle, first.'

'Suppose, now – this is merely a supposition, you know – suppose you could find a ledge that would yield, say, a hundred and fifty dollars a ton – would that satisfy you?'

'Try us once!' from the whole party.

'Or suppose – merely a supposition, of course – suppose you were to find a ledge that would yield two thousand dollars a ton – would *that* satisfy you?'

'Here – what do you mean? What are you coming at? Is there some mystery behind all this?'

'Never mind. I am not saying anything. You know perfectly well there are no rich mines here – of course you do. Because you have been around and examined for yourselves. Anybody would know that, that had been around. But just for the sake of argument, suppose – in a kind of general way – suppose some person were to tell you that two-thousand-dollar ledges were simply contemptible – contemptible, understand – and that right yonder in sight of the very cabin there were piles of pure gold and pure silver – oceans of it – enough to make you all rich in twenty-four hours! Come!'

'I should say he was as crazy as a loon!' said old Ballou, but wild with excitement, nevertheless.

'Gentlemen,' said I, 'I don't say anything – *I* haven't been around, you know, and of course don't know anything – but all I ask of you is to cast your eye on *that*, for instance, and tell me what you think of it!' and I tossed my treasure before them.

There was an eager scramble for it, and a closing of heads together over it under the candle-light. Then old Ballou said:

'Think of it? I think it is nothing but a lot of granite rubbish and nasty glittering mica that isn't worth ten cents an acre!'

So vanished my dream. So melted my wealth away. So toppled my airy castle to the earth and left me stricken and forlorn.

Moralizing, I observed, then, that 'all that glitters is not gold'.

Mr Ballou said I could go further than that, and lay it up among my treasures of knowledge, that *nothing* that glitters is gold. So I learned then, once for all, that gold in its native state is but dull, unornamental stuff, and that only low-born metals excite the admiration of the ignorant with an ostentatious glitter. However, like the rest of the world, I still go on underrating men of gold and glorifying men of mica. Commonplace human nature cannot rise above that.

A Gold Rush Glossary

Claim: The piece of land claimed by a prospector as his property and which he alone was entitled to mine. In the Klondike, the first man to discover gold on a creek that had not been located before was entitled to a **discovery claim**, as well as a claim for himself. The size of a claim varied in different goldfields but the most common size in the rich areas was 100 square feet (about nine square metres). Wooden stakes usually marked the boundaries between claims, hence the phrase **staking a claim**. If a miner moved onto someone else's claim illegally, the act was known as **claim jumping**.

Cradle: A trough, about three feet (a metre) in length, with narrow slats of wood nailed across it. At the head of the trough was a coarse sieve through which dirt was shovelled. Water was then poured into the trough and the entire cradle – or **rocker** – was rocked vigorously. The gravel would then be washed out at the foot of the trough, leaving gold on the slats. The cradle was later superseded by the **long tom**, a similar device about twelve feet (four metres) long, and by the **sluice**, in which a continuous flow of water was used.

Dryblowing: Because of the scarcity of water in the Australian goldfields, the cradle and sluice could not be used to mine gold. Australian prospectors therefore often separated the light earth from the heavier gold by 'dryblowing'. In the simplest method, a miner would gradually empty a dish of earth above his head into another at his feet, the dust and lighter material being carried away by the wind. A machine operated by a bellows was also used.

Fire-setting: In winter the ground in the Klondike goldfields froze solid, making conventional mining impossible. A solution was found by thawing the ground at night by lighting fires. With the use of 'fire-setting' – or **drifting** – mining could go on all the year round.

Fool's gold: Inexperienced prospectors often mistook iron pyrites (fool's gold) for the genuine article. It didn't take them long to learn that iron pyrites glitters, shatters under pressure and feels gritty between the teeth. True gold, on the other hand, shines evenly, flattens under pressure and feels smooth to the teeth.

Forty-niners: Strictly speaking, the name given to the gold hunters who travelled to California in 1849. It is used, though, to describe anyone who looked for gold in California during the years of the gold rush.

Fossick: A verb used in the Australian goldfields to describe the process of wandering from place to place in search of gold, often finding it in areas already unsuccessfully prospected by other gold hunters. **Fossickers** were solitary pioneer prospectors – the Australian equivalent of 'sourdoughs'.

Grub-stake: Money or supplies advanced to a prospector in return for a share of his findings.

Lode: A vein of gold-bearing ore which fills a well-defined fissure in rock. In a mine containing many lodes, the main vein is often called the **mother lode**.

Nugget: A lump of gold. Nuggets can vary enormously in size, and the largest ever found – the Holtermann Nugget – was discovered at Hill End, New South Wales, in 1872. It weighed 7560 ounces (214·32 kilograms). The largest nugget of *pure* gold to be discovered was the famous Welcome Stranger Nugget found at Moliagul in Victoria. It yielded 2268 ounces (64·296 kilograms) of gold.

Pan: A flat-bottomed pan with gently sloping sides was the basic tool of the prospector. Earth was put into the pan and water added. The miner swirled the pan so that the water washed lighter material over the edge, leaving the gold (if any) to sink to the bottom. The pan had other uses, too; one could use it for frying bacon and washing shirts, for instance. A mine, or an area which yielded gold, was often called a **pan out**.

Pay dirt: Earth, gravel or ore that is rich enough to make mining worthwhile.

Placer: A waterborne or glacial deposit of gravel or sand containing gold that has been eroded from the original rock and which can be washed out. **Placer mining** is the phrase used to describe the process of washing and dredging these deposits.

Prospect: A place where gold is sought or found, or a sample of earth which is tested for gold. It also means to search for gold, and a person who does this is known as a **prospector**.

Seam: A thin layer of gold between two strata of rock.

Sourdough: A name given to the original solitary prospectors of Alaska and the Klondike. The name derives from their habit of baking bread with 'sourdough': fermented dough saved from the previous baking in order to avoid the need for fresh yeast.

Strike: A discovery of a rich deposit of gold, hence the phrases: **strike it rich** and **lucky strike**.

River mining at Murderer's Bar

Bravo, Lola!

The goldfields of California and the Klondike, Australia and the Transvaal, attracted extraordinary characters of all kinds. Few were more extraordinary, though, than Lola Montez. She was born plain Marie Gilbert in Ireland in 1818 and, after an unhappy marriage, she achieved success as a dancer in London and Europe. By the time she arrived in California in 1853 she had, in swift succession, enjoyed three marriages, a trial for bigamy and scandalous relationships with the composer Franz Liszt and King Ludwig I of Bavaria. Lola's notoriety and legendary beauty did not guarantee her success in the music halls of the goldfields: her mining audiences were not impressed by her bad acting or her inept dancing, and even her famous Spider Dance – in which spiders made of cork, rubber and whalebone were shaken from her skirt – failed to impress the miners, who only laughed at her. After two years Lola grew understandably irritated by her lack of success and she left America – and a fourth husband – to seek her fortune elsewhere.

Lola joined the gold-hunters who were flocking to the new goldfields of Victoria in Australia. Perhaps the Australians would be more receptive to her charms. But her career there was as colourful as it had been in California: in Ballarat she horsewhipped a newspaper editor who had dared to denounce her Spider Dance, and her performance in Bendigo was interrupted when lightning struck the stage and destroyed much of the scenery. All the same, as William Craig remembered in his book *My Adventures on the Australian Goldfields* (1903), 'we had before us an astute and fascinating woman – one possessed of iron nerves as well as of unbridled ambition. Her frivolities ... are regarded with admiration by many of the diggers, and we hear such expressions as – "Isn't she a stunner!" "Bravo, Lola!" and ... "Oh, but you're a darlint, Loly!"'

By the time she died in New York six years later, Lola Montez had become a legend in her own lifetime.

Gold down under

The forty-niners did more than establish the prosperity of California and Nevada: they put their mining skills to use in other areas and other countries. A band of professional prospectors grew up, men who could identify promising fields and knew how to prospect and mine them efficiently. For many of these men the simple desire for wealth had been replaced by the urge to *find* gold; the discovery itself became more important and satisfying than any profit it might bring. From California they travelled north and west across America in their search for further deposits. And many of those who had come to California from abroad returned home eager to try their luck – and their mining expertise – in their own countries.

One of these men was Edward Hammond Hargraves, who had come to California in 1849 with other Australian gold hunters. The geological similarities between California and New South Wales convinced him that there was gold in Australia and he decided to return. His companions laughed at his theory. 'There's no gold in the country you're going to,' one of them said, 'and, if there is, that darned Queen wouldn't let you dig it.' To which Hargraves theatrically replied, 'There's as much gold in the country I'm going to as there is in California, and Her Most Gracious Majesty the Queen, God bless her, will appoint me one of her Gold Commissioners.'

Hargraves published an account of his eventual discovery in his book *Australia and Its Gold Fields*:

I then determined to visit Guyong, where I had been eighteen years before, and the neighbourhood of which I believed to be auriferous. I attempted to make a cross cut through the bush, and having travelled about eight or ten miles at nightfall, found myself on the Wellington road to the west instead of the north. After groping about in the dark for an hour or two, I found myself at Frederick's Valley, a district which has since become famous for its auriferous wealth. There I spent the night, and on the next day, the 10th of February, 1851, reached Guyong.

The landlady of the Guyong inn, Mrs Lister, had seen better days. I had known her during her husband's lifetime. She was now a widow. It occurred to me that I could not prosecute my plans efficiently without assistance, and that Mrs Lister was a person in whom I could safely confide, and she would probably furnish me with a guide and all the necessary implements. After dinner, therefore, I disclosed to her the object of my visit, and begged her to procure a black fellow as a guide to the spot I wished to visit first; for though this part of the world was many years back pretty well known to me, it is a matter of no small danger to attempt to penetrate alone the dense forests that cover the whole surrounding country. She entered with a woman's heartiness into my views, and offered me the assistance of her son, a youth of about eighteen years of age, who, she assured me, knew the country well. He was, therefore, made acquainted with my object, and, at my request, provided me with the requisite tools – a small pick, a trowel, and a tin dish for washing the soil.

After resting one day at Guyong, on the 12th of February I started thence, accompanied by young Lister. Our course was down the Lewis Pond Creek, a tributary of the Macquarie River. After travelling a distance of about fifteen miles, I found myself in the country that I was so anxiously longing to behold again. My recollection of it had not deceived me. The resemblance of its formation to that of California could not be doubted or mistaken. I felt myself surrounded

Gold and Gold-Hunters

Edward Hammond Hargraves went to California in 1849 with the other Australian gold hunters. The geological structure of the gold country there convinced him that there was gold in Australia. He searched along the Macquarie River in New South Wales and sure enough in Lewis Ponds he discovered gold. Within two weeks of the report of his discovery, in February 1851, six hundred men were at work in the area. The Australian gold rush had begun

by gold; and with tremulous anxiety panted for the moment of trial, when my magician's wand should transform this trackless wilderness into a region of countless wealth.

Still one difficulty seemed to present itself. There had been an unusual drought during the summer, which was now drawing to a close, and the creek, where we then were, was completely dried up. My guide, however, in answer to my inquiries, told me that we should find water lower down; so, following its course, we soon fell in with some rocks which contained a sufficient supply.

We now turned out our horses; and seated ourselves on the turf, as it was necessary to satisfy the cravings of hunger before I ventured on my grand experiment. Had that failed, but little appetite for food would have been left me.

My guide went for water to drink, and, after making a hasty repast, I told him that we were now in the gold fields, and that the gold was under his feet as he went to fetch the water for our dinner. He stared with incredulous amazement, and, on my telling him that I would now find some gold, watched my movements with the most intense interest. My own excitement, probably, was far more intense than his. I took the pick and scratched the gravel off a schistose dyke, which ran across the creek at right angles with its side; and, with the trowel, I dug a panful of earth, which I washed in the water-hole. The first trial produced a little piece of gold. 'Here it is!' I exclaimed; and I then washed five panfuls in succession, obtaining gold from all but one.

No further proof was necessary. To describe my feelings at that eventful moment would be impossible. What I said on the instant – though, I must admit, not warranted as the language of calm reflection – has been since much laughed at. And though my readers may renew the laugh, I shall not hesitate to repeat it, because, as it was the natural and impulsive expression of my overwrought feelings at the moment, so is it the only account I can now give of what those feelings were.

'This,' I exclaimed to my guide, 'is a memorable day in the history of New South Wales. I shall be a baronet, you will be knighted, and my old horse will be stuffed, put into a glass-case, and sent to the British Museum!'

At that instant I felt myself to be a great man. I was as mad, perhaps, at the moment, as Don Quixote was his life through; and, assuredly, my companion was as simple as Sancho Panza – for

Hints for prospectors

Many books were published which gave advice to gold-hunters about to journey to the new goldfields of America and Australia. The miners were able to learn from these where to find gold and how to mine it efficiently. Some of these books, like J. C. F. Johnson's Getting Gold, *published in 1897, also offered useful advice on how to survive the particular difficulties of life in the Australian outback:*

A BUSH BED

To make a comfortable bush bedplace, take four forked posts about 3 ft 6 in long and 2 to 3 in in diameter at the top; mark out your bedplace accurately and put a post at each corner, about 1 ft in the ground. Take two poles about 7 ft long, and having procured two strong five-bushel corn sacks, cut holes in the bottom corners, put the poles through, bringing the mouths of the sacks together, and secure them there with a strong stitch or two. Put your poles on the upright forked sticks.

PURIFYING WATER

There is not a more fertile disease distributor than water. The uninitiated generally take it for granted that so long as water looks clear it is necessarily pure and wholesome; as a matter of fact the contrary is more usually the case, except in very well watered countries, and such, as a rule, are not those in which gold is most plentifully got.

The best of all means of purifying water from organic substances is to boil it. If it be very bad, add carbon in the form of charcoal from your camp fire. If it be thick, you may, with advantage, add a little of the ash also.

PRODUCING FIRE

Everyone has heard, and most believe, that fire may be easily produced by rubbing together two pieces of wood. I have seen it done by natives, but I have never succeeded in the experiment.

The back of a pocket knife, or an old file with a fragment of flint, quartz, or pyrites struck smartly together over the remains of a burnt piece of calico will, in deft hands, produce a spark which can be fanned to a glow, and so ignite other material till a fire is produced.

Also he who carries a watch, carries a 'burning glass' with which he can, in clear weather, produce fire at will. Remove the glass of your watch and carefully three parts fill it with water (salt or fresh). This forms a lens which, held steadily, will easily ignite any light, dry, inflammable substance.

A SERVICEABLE SOAP

Wood ashes from the camp fire are boiled from day to day in a small quantity of water, and allowed to settle, the clear liquid being decanted off. When the required quantity of weak lye has been accumulated, evaporate by boiling, till a sufficient degree of strength has been obtained. Now melt down some mutton fat and, while hot, add to the boiling lye. Continue boiling and stirring till the mixture is about the consistency of thick porridge, pour into any convenient flat vessel, and let it stand till cool. If you have any resin in store, a little powdered and added gradually to the melting tallow, before mixing with the lye, will stiffen your soap.

Above: *gold hunters at Summer Hill Creek – just below Lewis Ponds on the Macquarie River*

Left: *a gold digger's camp*

Above: *the 'dryblowing' method of gold prospecting was invented to overcome the lack of water in Western Australia. The dirt was shaken in a mechanically agitated tray and the dust and dirt blown away leaving the gold particles (if any) in the bottom*

Right: *Samuel Thomas Gill was the Australian 'artist of the goldfields'. His sketches give a vivid impression of life in the goldfields in the 1850s. Here the digger is having his gold weighed in the buyer's store*

the good youth afterwards told me, he expected I should obtain for him the honour I had promised.

Within two weeks of a newspaper report of Hargraves' discovery in February 1851, six hundred men were at work in the area. Two months later the mining population had swelled to two thousand. The rush had begun.

Off to the Klondike!

The gold rushes in the Fraser River and Cariboo regions of British Columbia in the 1850s and 1860s convinced many prospectors of the existence of gold further north in the snowy wastes of Alaska and the Yukon basin. It was not until 1880, however, that the discoveries by Juneau and Harris in Alaska stimulated active interest in the area. In 1886, finds on Forty Mile Creek, a tributary of the Yukon River, attracted prospectors from the south, and camps grew at Forty Mile and Circle City. In 1896, the region was transformed by major discoveries in Canada. On 16 August G. W. Carmack and two Indians, Shookum Jim and Tagish Charley, found rich deposits of gold in Bonanza Creek. This creek flowed into the Throndiuck (later, Klondike) River which was itself a tributary of the Yukon. Carmack staked his claim by blazing a small spruce tree with his axe and writing on it in pencil:

TO WHOM IT MAY CONCERN

I do, this day, locate and claim by right of discovery, five hundred feet, running up stream from this notice. Located this 17th day of August, 1896.

G. W. Carmack

The news travelled quickly to Forty Mile and Circle City, and miners rushed from there to the new fields. When Harry Ash, a bar-tender at Circle City, heard the news, he leaped over the bar and shouted to his startled customers, 'Boys, help yourself to the whole shooting match. I'm off to the Klondike!' The 'boys' did so before staggering off to the Klondike themselves. Ash became a successful saloon owner in Dawson City, which quickly grew where the Klondike flowed into the Yukon. For some time his prosperity was based on the fact that his bar possessed the only piano in the town.

In the spring of 1897 four thousand people flocked to Dawson. When the news reached Seattle and San Francisco in July, the last great gold rush began in earnest. By the spring of 1898 news of the finds had flashed round the world and it is estimated that 100,000 people set off to try their luck in the Yukon.

In his book *Klondyke: Truth and Facts of the New El Dorado*, A. E. Ironmonger Sola set out 'a few words of advice to the would-be Klondyker', advice that reveals a great deal of the particular difficulties of life in the diggings:

As we all know, the Klondyke district is, without doubt, the richest placer mining district ever discovered in the world, but if people will only sit down, think, and argue their chances of success in this new 'Eldorado', they will undoubtedly come to the opinion that their chances are about one in a hundred.

It is an easy matter for anybody to sit before his own fireside at home and mine a claim in the Yukon (in imagination), but the actual prospecting is a different thing altogether. Before beginning even to hunt for gold the aspiring miner must prepare himself for the long and tedious

The Alaska gold rush of 1898. Don't be too impressed by the well-established look of the main street in Nome. The façades concealed sagging corrugated iron and rotten plywood. There was no sewage system and it cost 10 cents to use the latrines – a lot of money at that time

trip to the fields, and this is a task that will tax the endurance and nerve of the most hardy. It means packing provisions over pathless mountains, towing a heavy boat against a five to an eight-mile current, over battered boulders, digging in the bottomless frost, sleeping where night overtakes, fighting gnats and mosquitoes by the millions, shooting seething cañons and rapids, and enduring for seven long months a relentless cold which never rises above zero and frequently falls to 80° below. Any man who is physically able to endure all this who will go to the gold fields for a few years, can, by strict attention to business, make a good strike, with the possibilities of a fortune. We will take as an instance a young, inexperienced man leaving England with just enough money to pay his travelling expenses and provide himself with a year's outfit suitable for the Yukon country.

He leaves London for Liverpool; takes the steamer from Liverpool to New York; from New York he goes to, say, Seattle, in Washington territory, or Victoria, and from there he takes the steamer to, in my opinion the best route, Dyea. He is landed at Dyea with all his goods and chattels. He pitches his tent, and wonders how he is going to take his outfit over the summit to the lakes. Before starting he has not thought of

Working a claim in the Klondike

all the obstacles which are thrown in his way, and as it is absolutely necessary for not less than two men to travel together, one man, in his own opinion, always knows better than the other one what to do, and the result is in a great many cases that before the journey is really started these men divide their outfits and their friendship is broken ...

Providing everything goes smoothly, and both men agree what to do, we will say that they arrive at Dyea in the middle of March, when the snow is on the ground. Before leaving Victoria or Seattle, it is necessary for them to procure sleighs, and, if possible, two or three powerful dogs. They then load their sleighs and commence the ascent up the Dyea River to the foot of the Chilkoot Pass. Arriving at the foot of the pass it is necessary to make caches on which to load the provisions. The camp is pitched at the foot of the pass, as much as possible of the load is hauled and cached so that the dogs cannot reach it, and then they return to the camp. Of course, it all depends on the size and quantity of the men's outfit, the number of trips they have to make, and after making numerous caches on the way to the summit, and reaching the top the whole outfit can again be loaded on and sleighed down the other side, a distance of not much over

Chilkoot Pass was a favourite Canada–US border crossing point for the Klondike gold miners and prospectors. This is the last resting-place before the final ascent. It is called 'The Scales' and here the miners' packs were weighed. The Indian packers charged $1.00 per lb and most of them carried about 100 lb (45 kg) at a time

nine miles to the head of the lakes, then sleigh down the lakes until you come to a big patch of timber suitable for boat building purposes. Your camp is then pitched, your lumber sawed, and your boat built.

After having everything in readiness you may have to remain in camp for some little time until the ice breaks up in the lakes. A great mistake is often made by enthusiastic gold seekers in following the ice jamb too closely. Numbers of men have lost their lives from being caught in the ice and the boat being upset. I should advise that the ice have at least twenty-four hours' start. Then jump in your boat, and by exercising care and judgement, especially when nearing the different rapids, the trip can be made very easily and pleasantly.

This young Londoner arrives at Dawson City, where every temptation of a mining camp is open to him – all kinds of gambling devices, men willing at any time to pick a quarrel, women of all kinds and descriptions. He, of course, spends a few days in Dawson City before making up his mind to go out in the mountains and look for gold.

To prospect for gold he will have to pole his

75

boat up swift rivers, take a pack on his back and go up the most likely-looking creeks that he thinks will contain gold. After he finds a small amount of surface gold in the creek, he stakes out a claim and returns to Dawson City to record that claim, perhaps being distant a hundred miles from the town. He then returns to his claim and erects a log cabin before the snow falls.

After the snow is on the ground, and the river frozen up, he loads his supplies, stove, tools, etc., on his sleigh, and breaking a trail through the deep snow on snow shoes, and after making sundry trips, he eventually is located on his own piece of property. By that time I should say it would be about the month of January.

He then has to chop his wood from the side hills, haul it down to the creek, and chop it up. He then commences to sink prospect holes to bed rock. Each hole taking him no less time than from eight to ten days, and in the event of the ground being very deep, he will have to erect a windlass, fill his bucket in the bottom of the hole, then crawl up the ladder to the top and haul up the bucket. This is very hard and unsatisfactory work for one man to attempt, and until the owner of the claim knows what the ground contains, he does not feel justified, neither is he able to, hire a man and pay him $10 to $15 a day.

After sinking say ten of these holes, right across the width of the creek, and finding no gold

GOLD!
The Land of Promise!
The Glittering Treasure Found at last!

that will pay him to work, he naturally retires to his cabin, and looks at his worthless piece of ground, takes stock of his provisions and finds that they are nearly gone, and begins to wonder what to do. He has no provisions left sufficient to enable him to strike off for the mountains again. A whole year of his time has been apparently wasted, and the only thing for him to do is to return to the trading post, and try and get work of some kind, and scrape together enough money to enable him to buy another year's outfit ...

Experienced men have found that the provisions a man ought to lay by before starting on the overland journey from Juneau, at which place they can be best purchased, are somewhat as follows for one man for two months:

40 lbs flour	Matches
5 lbs baking powder	Mustard
24 lbs bacon	Cooking utensils and dishes
18 lbs beans	Frying pan
30 lbs dry fruit	Water kettle
12 lbs desiccated vegetables	Tent
8 lbs butter	Yukon stove
20 lbs sugar	Two pair good blankets
12 cans of milk	One rubber blanket

5 lbs tea	Bean pot
5 lbs coffee	Two plates
2 lbs salt	Drinking cup
12 lbs ham	Tea pot
10 lbs cheese	Knife and fork
20 lbs corn meal	Large cooking pan
Pepper	Small cooking pan

These are simply for sustenance. In addition, the traveller will find it necessary to build his own boat with which to thread the chain of lakes and rivers leading to the gold basin. He will need the following tools:

Jack plane	5 lbs of five-eighths rope
Whip saw	Pick
Two hand saws (cross-cut and rip)	Shovel
Draw knife	Gold pan
Axe	10 lbs 6d wire nails
Hammer	10 lbs 8d wire nails
Hatchet	10 lbs 12d wire nails
Pocket rule	Square
3 lbs oakum	Pencils
5 lbs pitch	Chalk

He will also find that he must have some protection against the deadly assaults of gnats and mosquitoes, which fill the air throughout Alaska; that he will have to be provided for mountain climbing and for protection against snow blindness, which is one of the most demoralizing afflictions that can befall the traveller over the snow-covered passes, so he will need:

Mosquito netting	Snow glasses
One pair crag-proof hip boots	Medicines

These are the provisions necessary for a miner, and whether he will need more for his journey depends somewhat upon the manner in which he travels ...

One word of advice to the young people who have only sufficient money to take them into that country – I should advise them to take the few hundred pounds that the trip would cost them and invest it in a sound legitimate Yukon Corporation. They will then reap the benefit without suffering the numerous hardships they would have to endure had they gone to work in the mines themselves.

The severity of the country and its climate probably deterred more people than did Sola's wise advice, but, even so, about forty thousand people finally completed the incredible journey to the Klondike.

The Dead Horse Trail

There were various routes to Dawson and the diggings, but all were long and arduous. Some miners took the 'Rich Man's Route' by ship to the Bering Sea port of St Michael and then up the Yukon by steamer. Others struggled overland from Edmonton and British Columbia but many died in the swamps and forests. The most popular route was by boat up the Pacific coast to the ports of Skagway and Dyea and from there over the coastal mountains to the Yukon river.

From Skagway, the gold hunters fought their way along the notorious Dead Horse Trail to the White Pass which would take them over the mountains. This route acquired its name from the heavily laden mules and horses which were driven up the mountains by the miners. Thousands of horses died from exhaustion and disease on the way. Few of the men knew how to handle animals, all were determined to reach the Klondike at any price. The price was usually an animal's life. Young Jack London, later to write *White Fang* and *The Call of the Wild*, travelled to the Klondike to search for gold

The notorious Dead Horse Trail. Thousands of horses and mules died of exhaustion and disease along this punishing trail

and, in one of his stories, recalled the ordeal of the Dead Horse Trail:

The horses died like mosquitoes in the first frost and from Skagway to Bennett they rotted in heaps. They died at the rocks, they were poisoned at the summit, and they starved at the Lakes; they fell off the trail, what there was of it, and they went through it; in the river they drowned under their loads or were smashed to pieces against the boulders; they snapped their legs in the crevices and broke their backs falling backwards with their packs; in the sloughs they sank from fright or smothered in the slime; and they were disembowelled in the bogs where the corduroy logs turned end up in the mud; men shot them, worked them to death and when they were gone, went back to the beach and bought more. Some did not bother to shoot them, stripping their saddles off and the shoes and leaving them where they fell. Their hearts turned to stone – those which did not break – and they became beasts, the men on the Dead Horse Trail.

An alternative route was over the Chilkoot Pass from the port of Dyea. This trail was too precipitous for animals and the miners were forced to carry their own loads. All through the winter of 1897 an endless line of men trudged to the summit, bent double under their packs. Among these men was Alexander MacDonald, who described the experience in an article for *Blackwood's Edinburgh Magazine* in 1899. With his Scottish companions, Mac and Stewart, a black mastiff called Dave, and a band of paid 'packers' to help carry the loads, MacDonald set off for the Chilkoot Pass:

Our tent was struck before daybreak ... and all our goods lay scattered in 50 lb sacks on the top of the snow. Leaving my companions to arrange matters and choose their respective loads, I went off to gather my pack team. I had some difficulty in rousing them: they were not at all anxious for the job, and if it had not been for the promise given the night before by their leader, I believe I should not have got one of them, even at their own extravagant price. They, however, got ready and came, sullenly enough, to our camping-ground to get their burdens. Most of them drew aside two fifties and at once proceeded to fix them into their pack-straps. One got our three sleighs as his load, while another contented himself with the stove and blankets.

Before their arrival on the scene Mac had packed for himself the tent and two fifties. 'A'm no gaun to be beat by ony man,' he grunted, as he adjusted his pack-straps to his satisfaction; and Stewart, not wishing to be excelled, surreptitiously undid his pack, which had contained the orthodox weight, and inserted another sack. 'If he can dae it, a' can dae it,' he remarked firmly; and no remonstrance of mine had any effect. Even Dave was requisitioned, and had all the cooking utensils strapped to his broad shoulders. As for myself, I carried my snow-shoes, three rifles, and all the ammunition – the latter no trifle – yet altogether my load was the lightest, and allowed me more freedom of movement than was possible to the others.

At eight o'clock we started: the chief packer went first; I followed with Dave at my heels, struggling nobly with his load; then came Mac and Stewart, while the main body straggled erratically behind. If the route to Sheep Camp was bad, the continuation to the base of the summit was a hundred times worse. The mountains gradually closing in on each side, we were forced to keep in the river-bed, and move upwards over its almost dry rocky channel as best we could. The acclivity was now exceedingly steep and seemed to lead right into the clouds; and as we slowly climbed, stopping every few hundred yards to rest, I wondered if the 'Summit' could be much more difficult. Great glaciers hung all around, and their enormous masses of blue ice stretched half-way down the mountains. No trace of vegetation was visible: truly it was a scene of the most extreme desolation.

After three hours of very hard work we reached the scales, as the base of the 'Summit' is called. The last climb was over the summit of the joining ridge of the Great Barrier Ranges that unite at this point, and from which many lesser spurs radiate.

For nearly 1000 feet the frowning barrier rose at an angle of almost 90°. No place for foothold could be seen, and the snow had covered any markings that might have been there previously. The snow was falling in large soft flakes as we sat down to rest before making the final effort, and the sound of the wind whistling fiercely above came to our ears as a soft sighing moan of varying cadence.

A few minutes passed in contemplation, and we started to the seemingly impossible task before us. The chief packer went first to pick out the snow-covered trail, but this he found to be impossible, owing to the depth of snow on the ledges. Several unsuccessful attempts were made, and my pack team began to show evident signs of mutiny: some were even prepared to return to Sheep Camp. Just then Dave scrambled past us, his pots and pans rattling furiously as he leapt upwards, and in a short time he was well above us, slowly yet surely getting nearer to the top.

'Hurrah! The dog's found it,' shouted the chief packer, who had been anxiously watching Dave's progress. 'Come on, boys, before his trail is covered;' and he was soon leading the way after Dave, I following in his tracks ...

With hands and feet clutching at the snow-covered rocks, and straining every nerve to keep from falling backwards, we struggled up the face of the awful mountain. At times we had to depend on strength of arm alone to drag ourselves over the jutting crags that stood out above

The Mounties had a customs post at the top of Chilkoot Pass. They forestalled smuggling of whisky, tracked down murderers, thieves and gamblers, and found lost travellers. They even carried mail to the scattered goldfields. Animals could not climb this steep slope and throughout the year an endless number of men trudged to the summit carrying their packs

us at intervals; and occasionally, when no foothold or chance crevice offered itself, progress could only be made by lying flat against the snow and writhing upwards until some welcome projection appeared to aid us. We seemed to make scarcely any progress, and when an hour had passed we were not more than half-way to the top; but so steep had been the ascent that a stone could be dropped to the point from which we started. A little more than half-way up the mountain we came to a small cave, and out of a fissure in its rocky floor gurgled a stream of crystal water. Here we rested for a few minutes and then started again to our difficult task.

It was getting late in the afternoon, and I was much afraid that darkness would be on us before we reached our destination. This way, then that way, in every conceivable manner, we twisted and zigzagged. Now we came to a narrow snow-covered ledge only a few inches in width, over which we moved carefully, not daring to look down: again a small glacier presented its slippery surface, and to it would succeed the usual stiff climb over snow-covered rocks ...

As we neared the top the whistle of the wind increased in shrillness and the air grew keener, and two hours after leaving the scales, amid blinding showers of snow, we arrived at the height of the notorious Chilkoot Pass. We floundered on through the snow, first into a small hollow, then over another sharp ascent, now called the second summit, and at last we looked down on the other side. Our pack team gave a yell of delight which I echoed heartily, and Mac and Stewart betrayed the depth of their emotion by muttered ejaculations of extraordinary fervour. The descent on this side was fairly steep, but without rocks, and an even depth of snow spread downwards into the mists below. The packers undid their loads and let them roll, while they themselves lay down on the snow and rolled after. My load of rifles, &c., prevented me joining in this exercise, so I had to be content with the more commonplace method of walking down on my snow-shoes.

We must have descended about 500 feet before reaching what in the dusk appeared to be a level table-land. It was almost dark when we got down, and my pack team departed hurriedly to get back over the summit before nightfall, and we three were left alone in an awful solitude.

St Patrick's Day at All Gold Creek

The lives of miners in the Klondike and their methods of working were dictated by the harsh landscape and weather. During the freezing winter, which lasted from September to June, mining operations were hampered by frozen ground and a lack of running water; in the continuous daylight of the brief summer, the intense heat and swampy conditions presented additional problems. Colourful and exciting Dawson City provided distraction for some, but most miners worked many miles from the town with only neighbouring diggers and small camps to provide companionship and relaxation. Despite their isolation, many miners contrived to make their own entertainment. National festivals were of particular significance to foreign diggers far from home and, in his autobiography, *The Hard Road to Klondike*, the Irishman Michael MacGowan tells how St Patrick's Day was celebrated during his time there:

The Irish always respected St Patrick's Day even out there in the wilds of the north. Even if his life depended on it, no man would do a stroke of work on that day. There was a fine spirit among all the men and no matter how much it discommoded them, they all behaved the same on that feast-day.

I well remember one St Patrick's morning that we were all out there and we had resolved the previous night that we would do no work next day. We were going to walk about five or six miles down the valley on a sort of pleasure trip. We knew that there would be a big crowd of people in the village. All the miners were used to relaxing there. As well as those, there were wealthy men there who had made plenty of money and who had men working for them up in the hills. They had nothing to do but to go up now and again and see that the men were working away. And this village in the valley below us was the sort of common recreation place; and that's where we had planned to spend St Patrick's Day ...

I was out at the side of the cabin this St Patrick's morning filling a can with snow. As I stood there, suddenly I thought I heard pipe-music in the distance. At first I thought it was a dream but in a short while I heard it again. I straightened up then as to hear it better but as luck had it, didn't the piper stop playing as soon as I was in a position to listen properly. It was some time before he started up again but when he did he seemed to be closer and the music was clearer; and wasn't the tune he was playing 'St Patrick's Day'. I'd say that by then the piper was three or four miles away up in the hills behind us; there, then, was I, three thousand miles from home but, in the time it would take you to clap your hands, I fancied I was back among my own people in Cloghaneely. My heart leaped up with so much joy that I was sure it was going to jump out of my breast altogether.

I ran back into the cabin and told my friends what was happening. They came out and ... everyone waited there until we felt the piper was coming near to us and then we all went out to meet him. Nobody was fully clothed and half of us hadn't eaten at all but our blood was hot and despite the frost none of us felt the cold a bit! When we met him, we carried him shoulder-high for a good part of the way back. He was brought into our cabin and neither food nor drink was spared on him. And it was still early in the day.

When everyone was ready, he tuned his pipes and off we went four abreast after him like soldiers in full marching order. There wasn't an Irish tune that we had ever heard that he didn't play on the way down the valley. Crowds of people from other countries were working away on the side of the hill and they didn't know from Adam what on earth was up with us marching off like that behind the piper. They thought we were off our heads altogether but we made it known to them that it was our very own day – the blessed feast-day of St Patrick. On we marched until we came to the hotels and we went into the first big one that we met. Without exaggeration, I'd say that there were up to six hundred men there before us – men from all parts of the world. We were thirsty after the march and, though we hadn't a bit of shamrock between us, we thought it no harm to keep up the old custom and to wet it as well as we were able.

We had a couple of drinks each and, as we relaxed, I stood up and asked the piper to tune up his pipes and play us 'St Patrick's Day' from one end of the house to the other. The word was hardly out of my mouth before he was on his feet. As I mentioned, there were people from all corners of the earth there and it was daring enough of me to do the like. The piper walked up and down and nobody interfered with him but I noticed that there was one man standing in front of me with a very disgruntled look on his face. He was a tall thin bony man about six feet in height if he was an inch. His face was sallow and he had two wild eyes and a nose with a hook on it ... Anyway, as he heard the tune from the piper, he got a glint in his eye like you'd see in the eye of an old codfish thrown into a dark corner some night. He had thick heavy lips also and, as he got agitated, the lower lip would fall just like the lip of a cow trying to pick up the last grain of oats from the bottom of a can ...

The piper was playing away and I knew from my man that it wouldn't be too long before he flew off the handle altogether. I was keeping my eye on him and watching the veins in his neck swelling with rage. Finally, as the piper passed him once again with the green ribbons hanging down from his pipes, the man grabbed at the ribbons to try and pull them off the pipes. I saw him and was so seized with anger that, without looking to one side or the other, I went straight over to him and hit him one blow of my fist behind the ear that stretched him out below me on the floor.

There was a bit of an uproar then and I thought something would start; but when the busy-body came to himself, what did he do only get up and walk out the door as quietly as you like, neither blessing nor cursing anyone. That was all and nobody that was present said that I had done a bad thing.

We stayed in the hotel and had a bite of food

and, when that was over, one of my companions said that he had to go down to another hotel to see the barman there. He had worked with him for a long time and knew him well. Off he went and he wasn't long gone until we saw him heading back towards us. We expressed surprise at his being back so soon but when he reached us we saw that he was in a bad humour. When we enquired what had happened, he said that the ruffian I had hit was in the other hotel and had attacked him as soon as he went in.

There was no need for another word. We all made for the door and headed for the other hotel. We were a fine body of strong young men and our company was increased by five other fine Irishmen that came with us from the hotel we had been in. On down we went with a man named Gallagher from my own parish leading the way. A fine brawny man he was that wouldn't turn the other cheek to any man in that Land of Gold. There were ten steps or so up to the door of the other hotel and on either side of the door were large glass windows. As we reached the top step, we saw the ruffian making for us with some of his own gang that he had collected. Gallagher was in front of our people and, as the man coming down got within striking distance, he lifted his fist and did nothing else to the ruffian but give him a huge clout on the chin that sent him backwards through the window. His friends walked on down without saying a word to us and it was well for them they they did so;

for if any man of them had opened his mouth, he'd have got the same treatment. We went ahead in then and some of the gathering there had hold of the man who had gone through the window. He was lying in a welter of his own blood on the floor ...

When we went into the hotel, we offered the hotel-keeper compensation for his broken window but when he heard the whole story of what had happened, he wouldn't accept a single penny at all. He was as proud of us as a cat would be with its kittens; he gave us food and drink and we spent a most entertaining evening in his place altogether. The man who had been felled went off and followed his own friends. Wherever he went to afterwards, we never laid eyes on himself or any of his friends from that day until we left Klondike.

As night fell, we all gathered ourselves together again and set off up the hill along the way we had come until we reached our own cabins again. We were tired out and it wasn't hard to make our beds that night. The piper spent the night with us and next morning he bade us farewell and went off to the back of the mountain where himself and two friends of his were working. A loyal good-natured Irishman, like thousands of others of his race he left his bones stretched under frost and snow, far from his people, out in the backwoods, where none of his own kith would ever come to say a prayer for his soul. We heard that he had been killed in one

85

of the shafts shortly after he had come to us to keep the Feast of St Patrick with his music in All Gold Creek.

MacGowan was one of the few diggers to make his fortune in the Klondike. He was twenty when he left County Donegal to seek his fortune in the United States. After working in an iron works in Pennsylvania and in the silver mines of Montana, he decided to try his luck in the Klondike, and by the time his claim was exhausted in 1901 he was a rich man. He returned to his village in Ireland, bought a large house and farm, and died a respected member of the community in 1948.

When MacGowan left the Klondike, its heyday was over. New Alaskan finds began to drain the population in 1903, and by 1906 the Klondike gold yield had dropped to a quarter of the amount produced five years earlier. Today, grass grows on the Dawson City sidewalks and the ornate saloons are silent and ruined.

Klondike was the last great gold rush: the closing pages of one of the most dramatic and exciting chapters in the story of man's hunt for gold.

Situations vacant

Few women lived in the mining camps during the early days of the California gold rush, and those who did were hardly respectable. Virtuous women, though, were able to take their pick from hundreds of miners who were anxious to marry and settle down. One enterprising lady had the bright idea of advertising for a husband in one of the local newspapers:

A HUSBAND WANTED

By a lady who can wash, cook, scour, sew, milk, spin, weave, hoe (can't plough), cut wood, make fires, feed the pigs, raise chickens, rock the cradle (gold rocker, I thank you, Sir!), saw a plank, drive nails, etc. These are a few of the solid branches; now for the ornamental. 'Long time ago' she went as far as syntax, read Murray's Geography and through two rules in Pike's Grammar. Could find 6 states on the Atlas, could read, and you see she can write. Can – no *could* – paint roses, butterflies, ships &c, but now she can paint houses, whitewash fences, &c.

Now for her terms.

Her age is none of your business. She is neither handsome nor a fright, yet an *old* man need *not* apply, nor any who have not a little more education than she has, and a great deal more gold, for there must be $20,000 settled on her before she will bind herself to perform all the above.

6. Gold robbers – and smugglers

Men were quick to appreciate the beauty of gold, and the power that it might bring them. They were quick, too, to recognize it as a source of evil: man's desire for the metal was so strong that he would go to any lengths to possess it. 'O cursed lust for gold,' wailed the Roman poet Virgil. 'To what dost thou not drive the hearts of men!' Honest hearts have always been prepared to earn gold, to mine gold, and, even, to make gold. Less noble spirits have always been quite content to steal it!

The great age of gold robberies began with the gold rushes. From the very beginning, the shambling mining camps of California attracted gold hunters who were well aware that there were less strenuous ways of getting gold than by prospecting for it. What was the point of working oneself to death in the diggings when a fortune in gold dust could be won in the gambling saloon or the dance hall? And those people who lacked the skill to find gold in this way were more than willing to use violence to possess it.

If prospecting for gold was a risky undertaking, then stealing gold was even more so! In the early days of the California rush, punishment was administered by the miners themselves. These men had risked their lives to reach California and had spent their days in desperate attempts to dredge a living from the creeks and gullies. Each grain of gold they found was treasured and hoarded, so it is hardly surprising that they did not look too kindly upon any of their fellows who tried to steal their hard-earned gold, and the punishment they administered to thieves was swift and violent.

How Hangtown got its name

E. Gould Buffum went to California in 1848 to find gold. In his book, *Six Months in the Gold Mines*, published in 1850, he described what happened at Old Dry Diggings when five men were caught in the act of gold robbery:

Never having witnessed a punishment inflicted by Lynch Law, I went over to the dry diggings on a clear Sunday morning, and on my arrival, found a large crowd collected around an oak tree, to which was lashed a man with a bared back, while another was applying a raw cowhide to his already gored flesh. A guard of a dozen men, with loaded rifles, pointed at the prisoners, stood ready to fire in case of an attempt being made to escape.

After the whole had been flogged, some fresh charges were preferred against three of the men – two Frenchmen, named Garcia and Bissi, and a Chilean, named Manuel. These were charged with a robbery and attempt to murder, on the Stanislaus River, during the previous fall. The unhappy men were removed to a neighbouring house, and being so weak from their punishment as to be unable to stand, were laid stretched upon the floor. As it was not possible for them to attend, they were tried in the open air, in their absence, by a crowd of some two hundred men, who had organized themselves into a jury, and appointed a *pro tempore* judge. The charges against them were well substantiated, but amounted to nothing more than an attempt at robbery and murder; no overt act being even alleged. They were known to be bad men, however, and a general sentiment seemed to prevail in the crowd that they ought to be got rid of.

At the close of the trial, which lasted some thirty minutes, the Judge put to vote the question, whether they had been proved guilty. A universal affirmative was the response; and then the question, 'What punishment shall be inflicted?' was asked. A brutal-looking fellow in the crowd cried out, 'Hang them.' The proposition was seconded, and met with almost universal approbation. I mounted a stump, and in the name of God, humanity, and law, protested against such a course of proceeding; but the crowd, by this time excited by frequent and deep potations of liquor from a neighbouring groggery, would listen to nothing contrary to their brutal desires, and even threatened to hang me if I did not immediately desist from any further remarks. Somewhat fearful that such might be my fate, and seeing the utter uselessness of further argument, I ceased, and prepared to witness the horrible tragedy.

Thirty minutes only were allowed the unhappy victims to prepare themselves to enter on the scenes of eternity. Three ropes were procured, and attached to the limb of a tree. The prisoners were marched out, placed upon a waggon, and the ropes put round their necks. No time was given them for explanation. They vainly tried to speak, but none of them understanding English, they were obliged to employ their native tongues, which but few of those assembled understood. Vainly they called for an interpreter, for their cries were drowned by the yells of a now infuriated mob. A black handkerchief was bound around the eyes of each: their arms were pinioned, and at a given signal, without priest or prayer book, the waggon was drawn from under them, and they were launched into eternity. Their graves were dug ready to receive them, and when life was entirely extinct, they were cut down and buried in their blankets. This was the first execution I ever witnessed. God grant that it may be the last!

It was this execution which gave Old Dry Diggings its notorious nickname – Hangtown. This name lingered on until the civic pride of later inhabitants caused the town to be renamed Placerville.

Black Bart

The dramatic events at Hangtown did little to deter those who hoped to make their fortunes by stealing gold. As the California rush continued and gold was found in increasing quantities, the robbery rate soared. A band of professional thieves grew up, men who had set their sights on more spectacular hauls. The most tempting targets were the stagecoaches which carried gold dust and bullion from the mines to the banks and refineries of the cities. These coaches were easy prey, for the rough California roads passed through deserted countryside with plenty of woodland to provide cover for the bandit. Communications were primitive and the robbers

Rough justice. There was no formal system of law in the goldfields. Punishment for wrongdoing was administered by the miners themselves. These men faced incredible hardships and spent all their time trying to dredge a living from the creeks and gullies of gold country: they dealt with thieves swiftly and violently

were able to make their escape well before the alarm was raised.

One of the most notorious robbers of the period was Black Bart, a man who had come to California to mine gold but who had turned to crime when his luck ran out. His exploits soon became legendary. The following account of one of Black Bart's ingenious hold-ups is taken from Garry Hogg's book, *Lust for Gold*:

He took a room one day at a hotel which he knew to be a regular staging-point for coaches on a gold run. He made a point of engaging the manager, hotel porter and other members of the staff in conversation so that he established himself properly with them from the start. When dusk began to fall, he mentioned that he was tired and proposed to go early to bed. He took his candle, said goodnight, and went upstairs. Once in his room, the first thing he did was to cut an inch or so off the *bottom* of his candle,

Gold robbers – and smugglers

which was a new one, and then replace it in its holder.

Later, he heard the stage-coach arrive; heard the passengers dining; heard the horses being changed in readiness for the scheduled departure, the time of which he had been careful to ascertain in advance. He slipped away unseen from his bedroom, crossed a field behind the hotel and jumped into a row-boat moored to a stake on the bank of a stream, crossed over, skilfully caught and mounted a horse grazing in a field, and set off in the direction of the ford some miles distant by which he knew the coach would have to pass.

It was a nicely calculated spot for a hold-up, for the stream bed was soft and the banks steepish. He waited as the coach drew near, swinging round the bend and slowing to negotiate the ford. Its wheels dug deep into the mud, the horses plunged and reared, the driver lashed at them in vain – for Black Bart as well as the opposite bank confronted them! The panic-stricken passengers unloaded their valuables, cursing the driver for being such a fool as to land them in such a predicament; and the solitary horseman galloped off into the darkness with the sound of their curses in his ears.

Long before the stage-coach had been extricated from the mud, reversed, and driven back to the hotel, Black Bart was back in his room, his profitable haul stowed among his baggage. He had the good sense to realize that if he were to show no interest in the tumult raised by the returned, despoiled travellers it might look suspicious. He therefore picked up his candle and descended the stairs, mildly inquiring as to the cause of the disturbance. The driver, almost beside himself with rage and frustration, unwisely shouted: 'That's the man who held up my coach! I know his beard.'

Black Bart smiled indulgently at this irrational outburst and raised an inquiring eye at the manager with whom, not so many hours before, he had been chatting, and at the hotel porter, from whom he had received his new candle.

'Nonsense,' said the manager, stoutly. 'I was talking with this gentleman myself only an hour ago, and saw him go upstairs to bed with his candle.'

Black Bart yawned, and pointed to his candle, the length of which clearly showed how long it had been burning. The stump he had providently cut off its base he had been careful to throw into the stream. He did not bother to refute what the angry driver had said: it was beneath the dignity of a respectable hotel guest. He offered his commiserations to the unhappy passengers, expressed the hope that the remainder of their journey would be uneventful, and betook himself to his bedroom once again.

Black Bart was eventually caught and imprisoned in the San Quentin Penitentiary. On his release, he announced that he would never steal again, but it wasn't long before further dramatic stage-coach robberies suggested that Black Bart's change of heart hadn't lasted very long.

The ordeal of Ellen Clacy

Gold robbery flourished too in the gold regions of Victoria and New South Wales. The Australian countryside offered splendid opportunities to the 'bushrangers' – men whose time and energy were devoted solely to the task of relieving miners of their hard-earned gold! These bandits lacked the finesse and style of men like Black Bart: many of them were convicts who had escaped from penal settlements and others were criminals who had served their sentences and who were now earning a living in the only way they knew. They roamed the outback singly or in bands, searching for likely victims. The most likely victims were usually miners returning to Melbourne and Sydney from the diggings.

A young Englishwoman, Ellen Clacy, has told the story of her own experience at the hands of bushrangers in her book *A Lady's Visit to the Gold Diggings of Australia in 1852–3*. Ellen came to Australia with her brother when he decided to 'fling aside his Homer and Euclid' and try his luck in the goldfields of Victoria. They joined forces with four other Englishmen and were lucky enough to be quite successful at the Bendigo diggings. Well satisfied with their venture, the party decided to return to Melbourne, taking with them a ten-year-old girl called Jessie whose parents had died at the diggings. Their route took them through the Black Forest, a notorious haunt of bushrangers:

We were comfortably seated at our breakfast, discussing a hundred subjects besides the food before us, when a shrill 'Coo-ee' burst through the air; 'Coo-ee', 'Coo-ee', again and again, till the very trees seemed to echo back the sound. We started to our feet, and, as if wondering what would come next, looked blankly at each other, and again the 'Coo-ee', more energetic still, rang in our ears. This is the call of the bush, it requires some little skill and patience, and when given well can be heard a great way off. In such a place as the Black Forest it could only proceed from someone who had lost their way, or be a signal of distress from some party in absolute danger. We again looked from one to the other – it bewildered us; and again the cry, only more plaintive than before, came to us. Simultaneously the men seized their pistols, and started in the direction whence the sounds proceeded.

Jessie and myself could not remain behind alone – it was impossible; we followed at a little distance, just keeping our comrades in sight. At last they came to a halt, not knowing where to turn, and we joined them. Frank gave a 'Coo-ee', and in about the space of a minute the words 'Help, help, come, come,' in scarcely audible sounds, answered to the call. We penetrated about thirty yards further, and a few low groans directed us to a spot more obscure, if possible, than the rest. There, firmly bound to two trees close together, were two men.

At length one man was released, and so faint and exhausted was he from the effects of whatever ill-usage he had suffered, that, being a tall, powerfully made man, it required the united strength of both Frank and Mr L. to prevent his falling to the ground.

Jessie and myself were standing a little apart in the shade, as if spellbound.

The second was soon set at liberty, and no sooner did he feel his hands and feet free from the cords than he gave a loud, shrill 'Coo-ee'.

A shriek burst from Jessie's lips and before anyone could recover from the bewilderment it occasioned, four well-armed men sprang upon our startled party.

Capture of bushrangers at night by Gold Escort Company police

The wretch who had been reclining in Frank's arms quickly found his feet, and, ere Frank could recover from his surprise, one heavy blow flung him to the ground; whilst the other twined his powerful arms round Mr L. and, after a short but sharp struggle, in which he was assisted by a fellow-villain, succeeded in mastering him.

It was a fearful sight, and I can hardly describe my feelings as I witnessed it. My brain seemed on fire, the trees appeared to reel around me, when a cold touch acted as a sudden restorative and almost forced a scream from my lips. It was Jessie's hand, cold as marble, touching mine. We spoke together in a low whisper, and both seemed inspired by the same thoughts, the same hope.

'I saw a little hill as we came here,' said Jessie. 'Let's try and find it and look out for help.'

I instinctively followed her, and stealthily creeping along, we gained a small rise of ground which commanded a more extended view than most places in the Black Forest, and, but for the thickness of the trees, we could have seen our own camping-place, and the part where the ambuscade had been laid. From the sounds of the voices, we could tell that the ruffians were leading their prisoners to the spot where we had passed the night, and the most fearful oaths and imprecations could ever and anon be heard. Well might our hearts beat with apprehension, for it was known that when disappointed in obtaining the gold they expected, they vented their rage in torturing their unfortunate victims.

Meanwhile Jessie seemed listening intently. The time she had spent in the bush and at the diggings had wonderfully refined her sense of hearing. Suddenly she gave a shrill 'Coo-ee'. The moment after, a shot was fired in the direction of our late camp. Jessie turned even paler, but recovering herself, 'Coo-ee' after 'Coo-ee' made the echoes ring. I joined my feeble efforts to hers; but she was evidently well used to this peculiar call. On a fine still day, this cry will reach for full three miles, and we counted upon this fact for obtaining some assistance.

'Help is coming,' said Jessie in a low voice, and once more with increasing strength she gave the call.

Footsteps approached nearer and nearer. I looked up, almost expecting to see those villainous countenances again.

'Women in danger!' shouted a manly voice, and several stalwart figures bounded to our side.

'Follow, follow!' cried Jessie, rushing forwards. I scarcely remember everything that occurred, for I was dizzy with excess of pleasure. There was a short scuffle, shots were fired at retreating bushrangers, and we saw our friends safe and free.

The whole matter was then related to our preservers – for such they were – and I then learnt that when the bushrangers had marched off our party to the camping-place, they proceeded to overhaul their pockets, and then bound them securely to some trees, whilst one stood ready with a pistol to shoot the first that should call for help, and the others looked over the plunder. This was little enough, for our travelling money, which was notes, was kept – strange treasury – in the lining of the body of my dress, and here too were the gold receipts from the Escort Office. Every night I took out about sufficient to defray the day's expenses, and this was generally given into Frank's hands.

Enraged and disappointed, the villains used most frightful language, accompanied by threats of violence; and the one on guard, irritated beyond his powers of endurance, fired the pistol in the direction of William's head. At this moment Jessie's first 'Coo-ee' was heard; this startled him, and the shot, from the aim of the pistol being disarranged, left him unhurt.

'It's that d—d child,' muttered one, with a few additional oaths. 'We'll wring her neck when we've secured the plunder.'

One of the ruffians now attempted more persuasive measures, and addressing Mr L., whom I suppose he considered the leader, expended his powers of persuasion much in the following manner.

'You sees, mate, we risks our lives to get your gold, and have it we will. Some you've got somewhere or another, for you haven't none on you, got no paper from the Escort – you planted it last night, eh? Jist show us where, and you shan't be touched at all, nor that little wretch yonder, what keeps screeching so; but if you don't – ' and here his natural ferocity mastered him, and he wound up with a volley of curses, in the midst of which our rescuers rushed upon them.

When we came to talk the whole matter over calmly and quietly, no doubt was left upon our minds as to the premeditation of the whole affair. But for the watch kept, the attack would most probably have been made during the night.

Our timely friends were a party of successful diggers returning from work. They too had passed the night in the Black Forest – providentially not far from us. They accepted our thanks in an offhand sort of way, only replying – which was certainly true – 'that we would have done the same for them'. It was in endeavouring to assist assumed sufferers that our party fell into the ambuscade laid for them.

They waited whilst we got the dray and horses ready, and we all journeyed on together, till the Black Forest was far behind us. We saw no more of the bushrangers, and encamped that night a few miles beyond the Bush Inn. At this inn we parted with our gallant friends. They were of the jovial sort, and having plenty of gold were determined on a spree. We never met them again.

A remarkable and daring outrage

The bushrangers did not remain content for long with the easy pickings to be gained from small parties of returning diggers. Shortly after the Victorian goldfields were opened, the government established a Gold Escort Company whose task it was to guard and protect the wagonloads of gold which were regularly transported to Melbourne from the diggings. At first these armed escorts enjoyed a long immunity from attack and, lulled by a mistaken sense of security, the Company reduced the number of men who accompanied the convoys. This did not escape the attention of the eager bushrangers, and in July 1853 an attack was made on a gold convoy that at the time was regarded as 'one of the most remarkable and daring outrages recorded in this or any other country'.

This account of the robbery was given by one of the troopers who was escorting the convoy:

We were escorting gold and specie from Mac Ivor to Kyneton, via the road to Melbourne. When we reached about four miles on Mac Ivor side of the Mia Mia Inn, I saw Sergeant Duins, who was then riding in advance, motion with his hand to the right side of the road. I followed his motion, and that moment we received a volley of shots from a sort of mia-mia on the side of the road. I was not shot down in the first instance, and drawing my pistol, fired at a man, who fired at me at the same time. I received his discharge in the neck, jaw, and nose, and tumbled from my horse. When on the ground I noticed two men, one on each wheel; they drew the boxes (containing the gold and specie) out of the cart, when some other men lifted them up and conveyed them into the bush. Looking around, I saw Fooks, the driver, and trooper Froaswater lying on the ground. I asked them whether they were hurt, when Fooks replied, 'I am a dead man.'

Six escaped convicts had been responsible for the attack, and five of them were arrested by the police shortly afterwards. There was no concrete evidence of their guilt, however, until the police offered a free pardon and £500 to any man who would confess and

Right: *bushrangers were the scourge of the Australian gold diggers. Shortly after the Victorian fields were opened the government set up a Gold Escort Company to guard the shipments of gold on their way to Melbourne from the diggings. Even this didn't stop the bushrangers and after one particularly daring raid the security guard was replaced by soldiers*

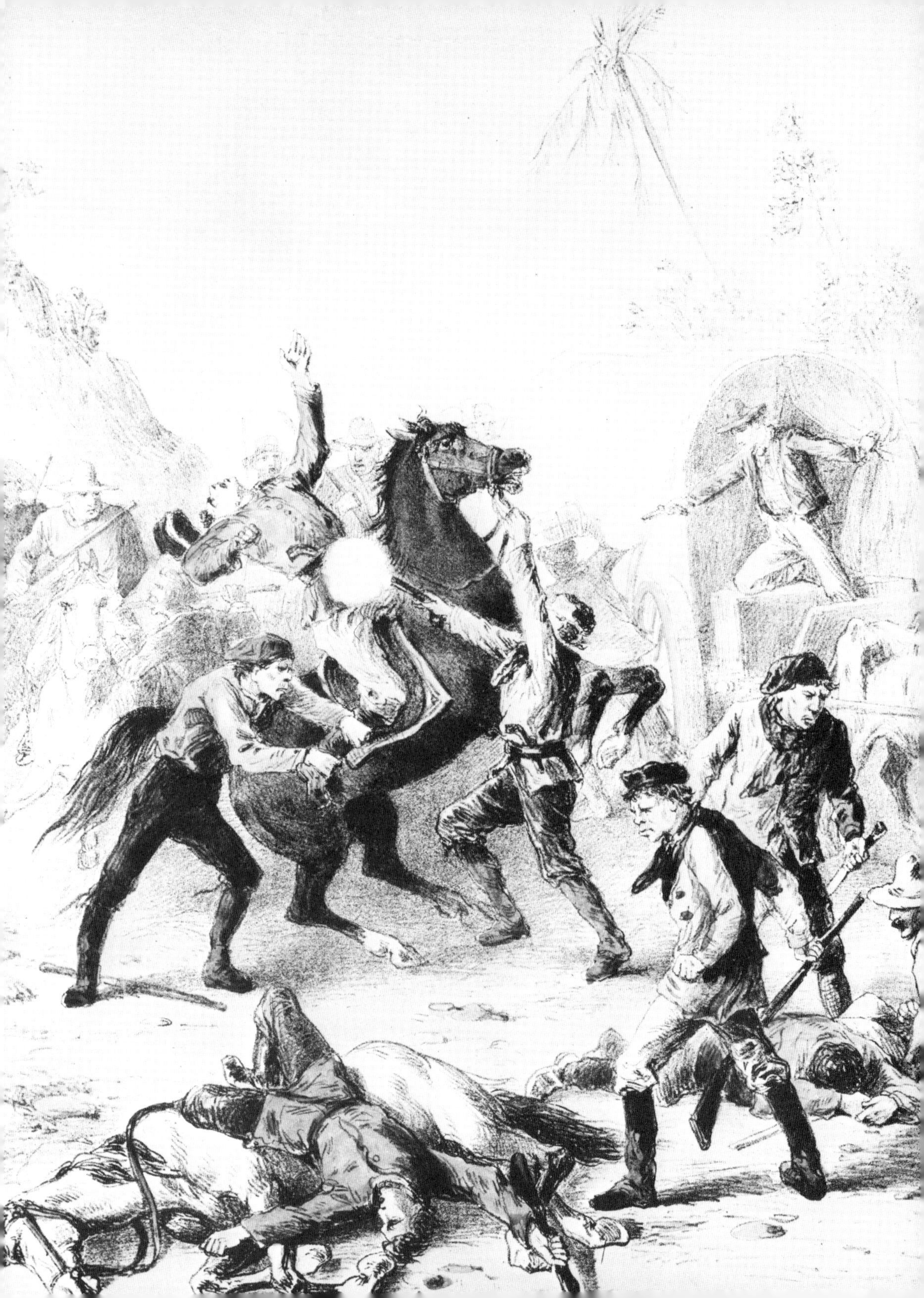

identify his accomplices. One of the bushrangers, George Francis, accepted this bribe. Then, either by accident or design, Francis was locked in a cell with the men he had betrayed, among them his brother. It is easy to imagine the scene in that cell as the arrested robbers were confronted with the man who had given them away. But no one knows what took place there. What we do know is that Francis took advantage of the carelessness of the warders and cut his throat with a razor.

When George Francis died he took with him the Crown case against his accomplices, and their conviction seemed unlikely. But John Francis, horrified by his brother's suicide, turned Queen's Evidence in his place, and the men were brought to trial.

George Wathen recorded John Francis's evidence – and that of the trooper – in his book *The Golden Colony*:

My name is John Francis, and I arrived in Van Diemen's Land under a sentence of ten years' transportation. My sentence has not yet expired, but will in September. On the 20th July last, I left the Mac Ivor company with George Francis, my brother, George Wilson, George Melville, William Atkins, and Joseph Grey. I now recognize Melville, Wilson and Atkins as three of the party named. We went through the bush from the Mac Ivor towards the Mia Mia Inn, and stopped on the side of the road a few miles from the inn alluded to. We soon after heard the Private Escort coming up, and it was now between ten and eleven in the morning. Previous to this we arranged a few branches of trees, and placed two men behind, the rest of them (and I) being stationed behind trees about thirty yards higher up the road. I heard some person of the Escort cry halt, and on looking out I saw some of the troopers firing at the two men behind the branches. We then, the rest of us, rushed down to their assistance. We all challenged the Escort men to stand, when they refused, and fired on us, when a general fight commenced. I fired at the Escort troop and observed four of the troopers wounded; two of the latter escaped, and two of us – myself and the prisoner Wilson – followed them, calling upon them to surrender. They replied by shooting at us, and galloping away. I and Wilson then went down the road, and gathering up all the firearms we could see, we followed Atkins, Melville, Grey and George Francis, who preceded us into the bush, whither the boxes of gold had been carried, and we then took the gold out of the boxes. It was whilst I and Wilson were after the two men that the gold had been removed from the cart. Where the gold was taken out of the boxes was some 200 yards from off the road into the bush, and after doing so, we travelled about seven miles through the country that day, and camped in the bush.

We resumed our route on the following morning, having first divided the gold. We passed the second night by a river's side, on Mollison's run, and continued our route in the same direction, always keeping to the bush and avoiding the road. The next night we passed in the bush, near Kilmore, and then on the Sunday morning we all left together for Melbourne, but separated on coming to the Rocky Water Holes, Grey and George Francis accompanying me into Melbourne. That night we reached town, and proceeded to my house at Collingwood Flat, where I saw Wilson and Atkins, it being previously arranged that we were to meet there. They remained at my house all night. On the day before I was apprehended I saw the prisoner Melville, when he told me he was going to Mauritius. The prisoner Wilson, I, and my brother were to have started for England in the *Madagascar*, and we had accordingly engaged passages in that vessel. My wife and George Francis' wife were to go with us. The confession was voluntary on my part, and there was no inducement held out to me. After the confession,

Captain MacMahon told me that he would send me a free man from the colony, with my wife. On arranging for this attack, we had resolved, if possible, not to take human life; for we thought we could get the gold without firing.

Francis's evidence was enough to convict all the prisoners, and three of them were executed. From then on, the amateur troopers who had escorted the gold convoys were replaced by soldiers.

The great bullion robbery

Bullion robbery did not die when railways replaced the stage-coach and the gold convoy. Trains carried bigger loads of gold and therefore even greater wealth, and the gold robber was quick to adapt his methods to suit the greater difficulties and dangers presented by this new form of transport. The gangs became increasingly ruthless and did not hesitate to kill if necessary. The romance and glamour of robbers like Black Bart disappeared for ever.

One of the most dramatic train robberies took place, not in America but in England, when nearly two hundredweight of gold bullion was stolen from the London to Folkestone boat train in 1855. On the evening of 15 May, three large chests of bullion were loaded into the guard's van of the train. They were securely bound, and locked inside a safe which was secured with the most up-to-date burglar-proof locks. The guard was instructed not to leave the van until the safe had been transferred to the boat at Folkestone. But when the safe was eventually unlocked in Paris, it was found to contain not gold but lead shot.

The robbery had been devised with meticulous care. The man who planned it was William Pierce, who worked in the ticket printing office of the railway. He had enlisted the help of a professional criminal called Edward Agar to do all the dirty work. The following account of their plan and its execution was included by W. Sapte in his book *A Century's Sensations:*

When Pierce first proposed the 'business', Agar declared it impracticable – at any rate, unless an impression of the keys to the safe could be got. On Pierce saying that this difficulty might be got over, Agar next demanded how many others would be involved apart from themselves.

'Two besides ourselves,' replied Pierce. 'I have sounded Burgess, one of the guards, and the other man I could count on is Tester, stationmaster at Margate.'

Agar, on learning that such useful confederates had already been obtained, decided to undertake the enterprise, we know with what success.

About a year before the robbery, he and Pierce had gone to stay at Folkestone, where they remained about a fortnight, during which they went constantly to the harbour on the arrival of the train from London, or the boat from Boulogne, to try and discover what was done with the keys when bullion was passing through. On one occasion they were so fortunate as to see the safe opened, which was done by a man named Sharman. Thinking he might be useful to them, Pierce, through the medium of Tester, who had once been a clerk at Folkestone Station, obtained an introduction to him; but he found the young man what he described as 'no good'; in other words, too honest. The police seem to have become suspicious of Picrce and Agar, by reason of their so frequently hanging around the station, and so these worthies beat a retreat to London, where, however, they kept their attention concentrated on the nefarious scheme.

Still the prospect of getting an impression of the keys continued to be remote, until fortune unexpectedly favoured the conspirators. One of the keys of the safe got lost and the latter had to be sent to Messrs Chubb's to be refitted. Somehow Tester, who by this time had been promoted to a clerkship at London Bridge, was able to get possession of the new key, and he took it to a public house in Tooley Street where Agar, who had been previously advised, had the wax ready. So far so good. The next step was to get an impression of the key kept at Folkestone, and this was very ingeniously contrived.

Agar gave Pierce a quantity of sovereigns which the latter consigned to him at Folkestone. Agar was thus enabled to be present at the opening of the bullion chest with a sufficiently good pretext, and he very carefully watched the operation, which was performed by a clerk named Chapman. Agar, having received his parcel of gold, noted where Chapman placed the key, and later on he was able, by careful watching, to get an opportunity of securing it long enough to make the wax impression he wanted.

He next had some 'blank' keys made and filed them to the size of the impressions he had taken. This was a long operation, and he took seven or eight journeys under Burgess' auspices before he was able to make them fit the locks. At last he accomplished this, and then nothing was wanted but the opportunity of bringing off a grand coup. Here again, Tester's official position came in useful, he being able to advise the others when a considerable quantity of bullion would be travelling.

Nor was this all that was necessary. Burgess had to be in charge of the guard's van as well, and it was his business to give the final signal, a simple one, but quite enough for the keen ruffians on the watch. He was to wipe his face with his handkerchief, a very natural operation for a hard-worked man on a warm day.

After five or six fruitless attendances at London Bridge Station, the necessary conditions were fulfilled. The mail was going off with bullion worth getting on for £20,000, and the safe was in Burgess' charge. Taking first class tickets, Pierce, Tester and Agar passed on to the platform, and the last-named, seizing a favourable opportunity, jumped into Burgess' van, where the guard promptly placed a large apron over him in case anyone should look in.

The journey once commenced, Agar lost no time in setting to work. To use his own words: 'I opened an iron safe and took from it a wooden box, fastened by nails and iron bands, and also sealed ... I took from that box bars of gold ... I put the shot in the box instead. By this time we were nearing Reigate, and when we stopped there I gave the bag to Burgess. I heard Tester say, "Where is it?"'

So Tester, who left the train at this point, got clear off with the first instalment of the booty.

Afterwards, Agar opened the other boxes, removed their contents and, as before, substituted shot. This shot, be it said, had been previously purchased at the well-known Shot Tower, and had been carried into Burgess' van in innocent-looking carpet bags by unsuspecting porters at London Bridge. The gold secured, Agar fastened up the boxes, and re-sealed them with wax brought for the purpose, after which he locked the safe, which then presented absolutely no appearance of having been tampered with.

On arriving at Folkestone, Pierce joined Agar, and the two, with their bags full of the precious spoil, went to the Dover Castle Hotel, where they had a merry supper. They returned to town by the 2 a.m. train, and proceeded to put possible trackers off the scent by cab-rides to various termini in various vehicles. Finally they drove to Pierce's house.

The gold did not remain long here. Some small portions of it were carefully and judiciously realized, and then the bulk was taken to Agar's first floor room in Cambridge Terrace, Shepherd's Bush. Here, by removing the hearthstone and inserting firebricks, a rough furnace was made in which the gold was melted down in crucibles ... Once one of the crucibles upset and very nearly set the house on fire, the liquid gold running into the chinks and crevices of the floor.

Gradually the bulk of the gold was disposed of, the proceeds going fairly equally among the confederates, though Burgess and Tester seemed to have fared worse than Pierce, who, in addition, secured possession of the residue of unmelted gold, and stored it in a hole dug in his pantry.

At first it seemed as though Pierce and his accomplices would never be caught. The hue and cry slowly died down and, for two years, the four men lived comfortably on the proceeds of the robbery. But then Edward Agar was arrested for forging a cheque and was imprisoned in Newgate. Pierce promised faithfully to provide for Agar's girlfriend, Fanny Kay, but when it became clear that Agar would shortly be transported to Australia, Pierce conveniently forgot his vow. Fanny Kay didn't, though. She told Agar of Pierce's duplicity and he in turn denounced Pierce to the police and told them the full story of the robbery.

Gold in the sky

Nowadays gold bullion is usually transported by air, a form of transport that might be thought immune from the attention of thieves. But the ingenuity of the gold robber has not been inhibited by the aeroplane. In 1954 gold bullion to the value of £40,000 was stolen from a KLM van on its way to London Airport. In 1957, six hundred gold bars worth £20,000 were snatched from a British Airways van between the Waterloo Air Terminal and Heathrow.

These robberies took place on the ground but the events of August 1957 showed that gold isn't safe in the air, either. On 13 August, twelve boxes of gold ingots were loaded on to an Air France jet in Paris. When the plane landed in Geneva, only eleven were left. No one has ever discovered what happened to the missing box, and the ingots – worth £12,500 – have never been recovered.

The international jet is also the haunt of a different kind of criminal – the gold smuggler. In his book, *The Smugglers*, Timothy Green gives a fascinating picture of the curious world of gold smuggling and of

---

Right: *the modern gold smuggler is extremely inventive. Every article in this picture has been used to smuggle gold*

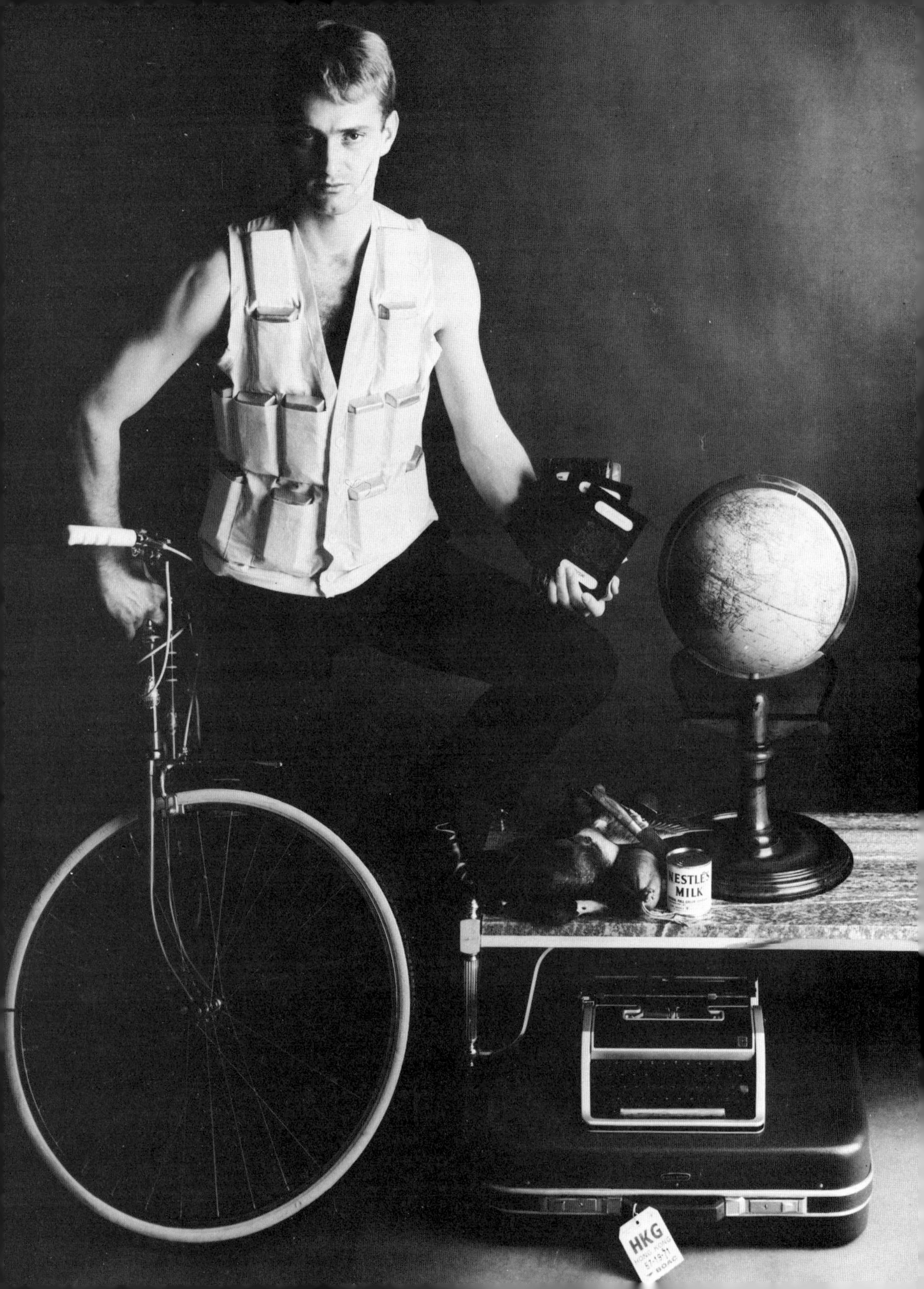
NESTLE'S
MILK
HKG
BOAC

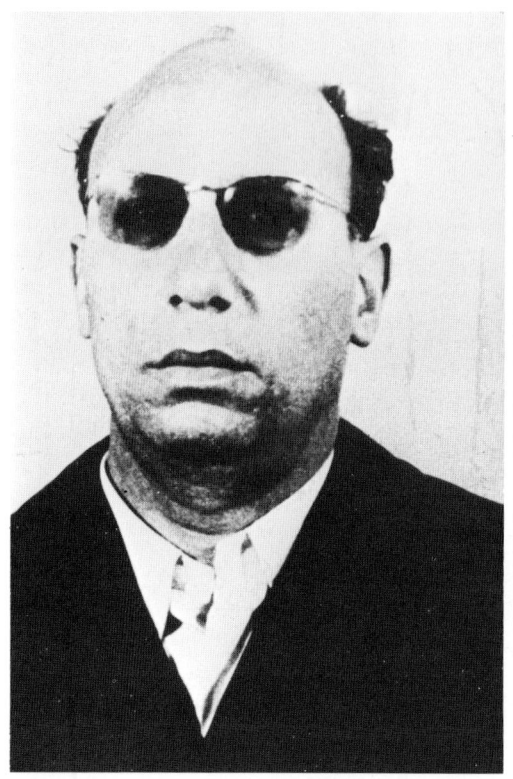

Above: *David Ventura was the leader of a gold-smuggling ring. He and his accomplices had hidden 260 gold bars worth 330 million yen in the bottom of 263 35-lb cans of motor grease to be smuggled into Japan*

Left: *an official examining the wing of a 1950 Buick taken off the* Queen Elizabeth. *A fifty-one-year-old American rag collector was arrested in New York when customs officials found 340 lb (154 kg) of gold bullion under the wings of his car. He said he had been offered $1 000 to deliver the car to Paris and knew nothing about the gold!*

Above: *some of the bars of gold taken from the bodywork of the car*

Right: *a customs official wearing a special belt designed to smuggle gold bars or precious stones*

Gold and Gold-Hunters

the men who organize and control the smuggling syndicates:

Gold smuggling calls for a great deal of stamina and costs a great deal of sweat. The favourite smuggling technique is to use a thin canvas or nylon corset, bearing thirty or more kilo bars of gold slotted neatly into rows all round the garment, strapped to the torso. Wearing it is a wearying experience. Suddenly it seems you are in a strait jacket, held down, restricted, unable to move. A latter-day Tutankhamen in a gold shroud. The weight of this golden waistcoat is crippling; it grips you like a vice, and knees buckle slightly. Sitting down is not much relief; trying to stand up again, while maintaining a casual air, becomes a feat of strength. Walking becomes a deliberate effort with careful strides to maintain equilibrium. 'Remember,' says the man handing out the jacket, 'that you can easily be knocked off balance if you are bumped or jostled in a crowd.' Just to ram home the point, he comes heavily across the room on a collision course; it is all too easy to collapse ungracefully. Which could be most embarrassing in the midst of a busy airport under the eyes of the authorities. And always at the back of the mind is the story of the German courier with the golden waistcoat flying from Geneva to the Far East, who died of a heart attack, caused by exhaustion, at Athens airport when his aircraft stopped to refuel.

With so many physical hazards en route – quite apart from the normal risk of detection by the authorities – gold smuggling has become, over the last twenty years, a specialized trade, second only, in terms of organization, to heroin. The main gold smuggling syndicates operating out of Europe, the Middle East and, to a lesser degree, Canada, handle between them $300 million to $400 million in gold a year; a turnover which would put them in the top hundred companies in Europe or America if they cared to publish their dealings. In any event their affairs are as well run as those of any giant corporation. Indeed for most of the leading smugglers, gold is simply a profitable sideline in their normal business as well established exchange dealers, import and export merchants or travel agents. Of course they have to be a little more discreet when it involves gold. As well as on the sweating couriers of international jets, the gold travels amid a clutter of goats and pilgrims on Arab dhows in the Arabian Gulf, or hidden in the engine casing of freighters outward bound from Hong Kong. One shipment of movie projectors into India in 1968 were ingeniously filled with canapé-sized bars of gold, while 560 cans of motor grease swung ashore in Yokohama were laced with over $1 million in gold ...

But why smuggle gold anyway? Logically, of course, the grip of gold in the hearts and minds of millions of individuals around the world is absurd. The metal has no intrinsic value. It is hard to imagine being cast up on a desert island with anything more useless than a bar of gold. But the basic motive for the ordinary man to hoard gold bars or gold jewellery is fear – and that at once casts logic aside.

The fear that dominates the gold hoarder may be of devaluation, of civil war or strife, of being kicked unceremoniously out of his country for political reasons or simply, as in India, of losing face because he cannot deck out his daughter with enough gold ornaments on her wedding day ... Around the world sixty-eight nations still permit their citizens to hold gold privately; the smuggler's market is the 145 nations that do not – or impose strict controls on the import of gold. In these countries fear can drive the black market price for gold up to ... twice the normal market price ...

Couriers come from every country in Europe and in recent years have ranged from an out-of-work dancer from Cardiff to students from Stockholm; from taxi drivers from Munich to Catholic priests from Milan (their robes are excellent for concealing gold). Women are equally welcome; they cannot carry quite so much gold, but they attract far less attention. Many couriers are wives, girlfriends, even mothers-in-law of established smugglers. Others are recruited through carefully worded advertisements in the personal column of *The Times* or other newspapers which hint vaguely at rewarding travel opportunities ... Couriers are expendable, but it can pay an organization with a turnover of perhaps $20 million a year to look after its employees when they are in trouble. The gold syndicates are always at pains to stress that they are not criminal outfits, that they are merely supplying a commodity that is prohibited by some quirk of local economic regulations. They go to considerable trouble not to recruit people with criminal records and are most ethical in all their business dealings. One well-known international smuggler, operating out of Brussels, was double-crossed in Pakistan and lost a major shipment of gold, which he had obtained largely on credit. He went to great lengths to raise the necessary capital to pay off his debt.

Even couriers who have been caught are not necessarily blacked. Indeed one Swiss courier had the doubtful distinction of being caught twice during 1968. He was first arrested by American customs in Seattle in February with thirty-two kilo bars of gold in a jacket beneath his shirt, when he was in transit from Vancouver, where he had taken delivery of the gold, to San Francisco, where he had a reservation on a trans-Pacific flight to Manila. He was posing as a representative of a Swiss duplicating firm. Six months later he was arrested again, together with a Chilean, coming into Hong Kong aboard the *SS Tarantel* from Manila. The two men had eighty-four kilo bars of gold between them, which they had picked up in Switzerland, carried in jackets by air to the Philippines and then tried to bring into Hong Kong by the highly unusual backdoor sea route from Manila (smugglers coming into Hong Kong normally come direct by air). On both occasions this Swiss courier had a veritable deck of airline tickets with him. In Seattle he had $2000 worth of tickets and a routing Geneva, Frankfurt, Nicosia, Istanbul, Beirut, Vancouver, Tokyo, Hong Kong, Manila, Djakarta and Bangkok. He had two Swiss passports, one issued in 1965 and already completely filled with visa stamps; the other issued in Hong Kong was already being filled up fast ...

A very experienced customs officer can pick out a courier, unless the latter is very skilful. 'You get an eye for them,' explained an officer in Hong Kong, 'look for how they bend down to pick up their suitcase, see how they stand when they wait in line.' One syndicate issues its couriers with tranquillizers to be taken just before landing to make them relax before customs inspection.

No one knows exactly how much gold is humped around the world each year on the sweating backs of the couriers, but it is certainly at least fifty tons of gold worth nearly $60 million. In one peak week in 1968 just before the gold crisis ... one Geneva group was sending twenty-five couriers a week to south-east Asia, sometimes eight of them travelling together on the same flight. Assuming each of them carried at least thirty kilos of gold (a very strong courier can take up to forty kilos, but the average is between thirty and thirty-five) that means this syndicate alone was shifting nearly three-quarters of a ton a week. This is by no means a record. One Beirut smuggler likes to recall how he once went out to the airport to watch the Panam flight to Hong Kong take off with sixteen couriers on board, with a total of half a ton of undeclared gold beneath their shirts. There was some speculation among the Beirut market as to whether or not the plane would get off the ground. It did!

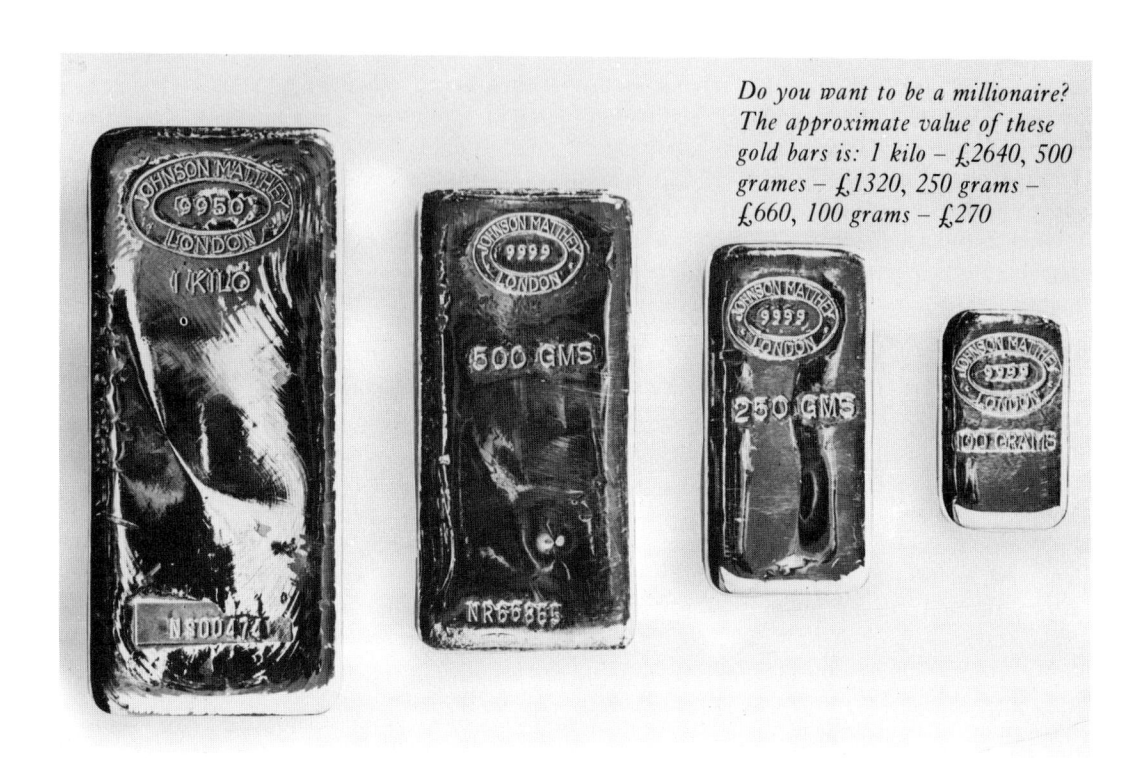

Do you want to be a millionaire? The approximate value of these gold bars is: 1 kilo – £2640, 500 grames – £1320, 250 grams – £660, 100 grams – £270

7. Hidden gold

A Yale University professor once remarked that 'nobody could ever have conceived of a more absurd waste of human resources than to dig gold in distant corners of the earth for the sole purpose of transporting it and reburying it immediately afterwards in other deep holes, especially excavated to receive it and heavily guarded to protect it'. He is right, of course, but logic and common sense play little part in the story of men's hunt for gold. Throughout the centuries they have fought to possess it and other men, in their turn, have fought to take it from them. Therefore it is essential to hide gold to ensure its safety, and the best hiding place is usually in the ground. Such hiding places may range from a tin box buried beneath the floorboards of a suburban house, to the vaults of the Federal Reserve Bank in New York City where over 14,000 tons of gold lie eighty-five feet (twenty-five metres) below ground. But, whether the gold is in a tin box or a guarded vault, the reasons for its burial are identical.

The most impressive hiding place in the world is the United States Bullion Depository of Fort Knox, where gold valued (in

1975) at £5,066,000,000 is stored in a massive structure of steel, concrete and granite, protected by a steel door weighing twenty tonnes and guarded by elaborate electrical devices and a force of over one thousand men of the First Mechanized Cavalry.

Only in novels – notably Ian Fleming's *Goldfinger* – have men attempted to steal the treasure of Fort Knox. Less spectacular hoards, though, have always excited the imagination and, throughout history, men and women have travelled the earth to locate and unearth golden treasure.

The tomb of Tutankhamen

Graves have always been a rich source of gold for both the robber and the treasure hunter. Ancient kings liked to take their gold with them when they died, and their tombs were often filled with the treasures that had pleased them in life. Such graves were usually plundered by alert grave robbers long before their discovery by archaeologists, but every now and again a discovery is made which can excite the imagination of the world. One such find took place in 1922 when Howard Carter discovered the tomb of the boy Pharaoh Tutankhamen. The tomb revealed a treasure of incomparable richness, and the value of the gold contained within it can never be assessed. Howard Carter wrote of the discovery in his book *The Tomb of Tutankhamen*. It is a vivid account which shows how the sober investigations of the archaeologist can be infected by the thrill and excitement of finding hidden treasure:

The day following (26 November) was the day of days, the most wonderful that I have ever lived through, and certainly one whose like I can never hope to see again ... Slowly, desperately slowly it seemed to us as we watched, the remains of passage debris that encumbered the lower part of the doorway were removed, until at last we had the whole door clear before us. The decisive moment had arrived. With trembling hands I made a tiny breach in the upper left-hand corner. Darkness and blank space, as far as an iron testing-rod could reach, showed that whatever lay beyond was empty, and not filled like the passage we had just cleared. Candle tests were applied as a precaution against possible foul gases, and then, widening the hole a little, I inserted the candle and peered in ... At first I could see nothing, the hot air escaping from the chamber causing the candle flame to flicker, but presently, as my eyes grew accustomed to the light, details of the room within emerged slowly from the mist, strange animals, statues, and gold – everywhere the glint of gold ...

I suppose most excavators would confess to a feeling of awe – embarrassment almost – when they break into a chamber closed and sealed by pious hands so many centuries ago. For the moment, time as a factor in human life has lost its meaning. Three thousand, four thousand years maybe, have passed and gone since human feet last trod the floor on which you stand, and yet, as you note the signs of recent life around you – the half-filled bowl of mortar for the door, the blackened lamp, the finger-mark upon the freshly painted surface, the farewell garland dropped upon the threshold – you feel it might have been but yesterday. The very air you breathe, unchanged throughout the centuries, you share with those who laid the mummy to its rest. Time is annihilated by little intimate details such as these, and you feel an intruder.

That is perhaps the first and dominant sensation, but others follow thick and fast – the exhilaration of discovery, the fever of suspense, the almost over-mastering impulse, born of curiosity, to break down seals and lift the lids of

Gold and Gold-Hunters

boxes, the thought – pure joy to the investigator – that you are about to add a page to history, or solve some problem of research, the strained expectancy – why not confess it? – of the treasure-seeker. Did these thoughts actually pass through our minds at the time, or have I imagined them since? I cannot tell. It was the discovery that my memory was blank, and not the mere desire for a dramatic chapter-ending, that occasioned this digression.

Surely never before in the whole history of excavation had such an amazing sight been seen as the light of our torch revealed to us ... The effect was bewildering, overwhelming. I suppose we had never formulated exactly in our minds just what we had expected or hoped to see, but certainly we had never dreamed of anything like this, a roomful – a whole museumful, it seemed – of objects, some familiar, but some the like of which we had never seen, piled one upon another in seemingly endless profusion.

Gradually the scene grew clearer, and we could pick out individual objects. First, right opposite to us – we had been conscious of them all the while, but refused to believe in them – were three great couches, their sides carved in the form of monstrous animals, curiously attenuated in body, as they had to be to serve their purpose, but with heads of startling

Below: *the antechamber of Tutankhamen's tomb – on the left the King's chariots, on the right pieces of furniture, and 'everywhere the glint of gold'*

Right: *the solid gold third coffin of King Tutankhamen*

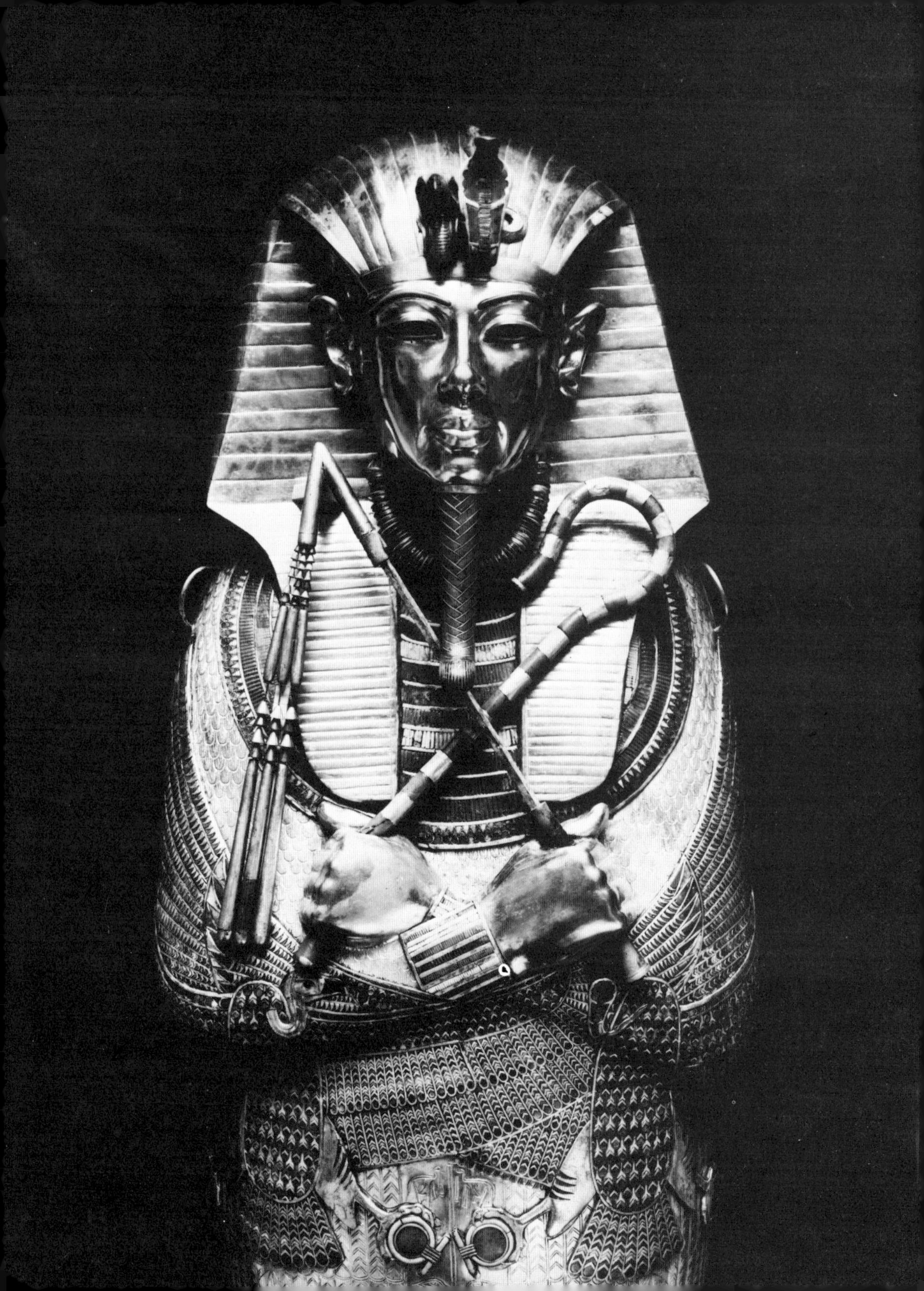

Gold and Gold-Hunters

realism. Uncanny beasts enough to look upon at any time: seen as we saw them, their brilliant gilded surfaces picked out of the darkness by our electric torch, as though by limelight, their heads throwing grotesque distorted shadows on the wall behind them, they were almost terrifying. Next, on the right, two statues caught and held our attention; two life-sized figures of a king in black, facing each other like sentinels, gold kilted, gold sandalled, armed with mace and staff, the protective sacred cobra upon their foreheads.

These were the dominant objects that caught the eye at first. Between them, around them, piled on top of them, there were countless others – exquisitely painted and inlaid caskets; alabaster vases, some beautifully carved in openwork designs; strange black shrines, from the open door of one a great gilt snake peeping out; bouquets of flowers or leaves; beds; chairs beautifully carved; a golden inlaid throne; a heap of curious white oviform boxes; staves of all shapes and designs; beneath our eyes, on the very threshold of the chamber, a beautiful lotiform cup of translucent alabaster; on the left a confused pile of overturned chariots, glistening with gold and inlay; and peeping from behind them another portrait of a king.

Such were some of the objects that lay before us. Whether we noted them all at the time I cannot say for certain, as our minds were in much too excited and confused a state to register accurately. Presently it dawned upon our bewildered brains that in all this medley of objects before us there was no coffin or trace of mummy, and the much-debated question of tomb or cache began to intrigue us afresh. With this question in view we re-examined the scene before us, and noticed for the first time that between the two black sentinel statues on the right there was another sealed doorway. The explanation gradually dawned upon us. We were but on the threshold of our discovery. What we saw was merely an antechamber. Behind the guarded door there were to be other chambers, possibly a succession of them, and in one of them, beyond any shadow of doubt, in all his magnificent panoply of death, we should find the Pharaoh lying ...

It was not until February of the following year, after the antechamber had been cleared and its contents examined, that Carter and his colleagues were able to set about the momentous task of investigating the guarded door.

My first care was to locate the wooden lintel above the door: then very carefully I chipped away the plaster and picked out the small stones which formed the uppermost layer of the filling. The temptation to stop and peer inside at every moment was irresistible, and when, after about ten minutes' work, I had made a hole large enough to enable me to do so, I inserted an electric torch. An astonishing sight its light revealed, for there, within a yard of the doorway, stretching as far as one could see and blocking the entrance to the chamber, stood what to all appearance was a solid wall of gold ... We were at the entrance of the actual burial-chamber of the king, and that which barred our way was the side of an immense gilt shrine built to cover and protect the sarcophagus ... So enormous was this structure (17 feet by 11 feet, and 9 feet high, we found afterwards) that it filled within a little the entire area of the chamber, space of some two feet only separating it from the walls on all four sides, while its roof, with cornice top and torus moulding, reached almost to the ceiling. From top to bottom it was overlaid with gold, and upon its sides there were inlaid panels of brilliant blue faience, in which were represented, repeated over and over, the magic symbols which would ensure its strength and safety. Around the shrine, resting upon the ground, there were a

---

Right: *the scene on the back panel of the golden throne of Tutankhamen. The king is seated and is being anointed with ointment by his wife*

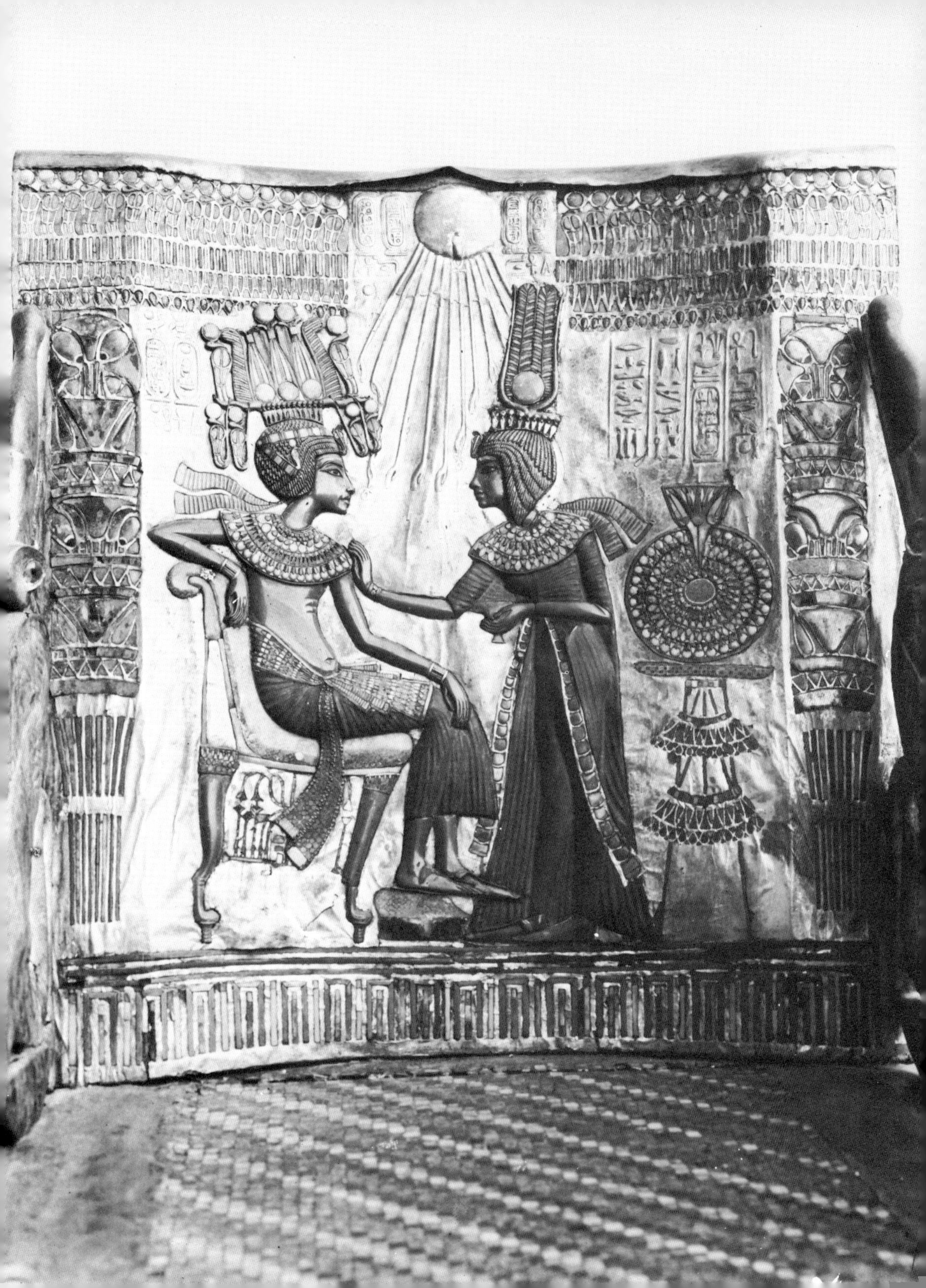

number of funerary emblems, and, at the north end, the seven magic oars the king would need to ferry himself across the waters of the underworld. The walls of the chamber, unlike those of the antechamber, were decorated with brightly painted scenes and inscriptions, brilliant in their colours, but evidently somewhat hastily executed ...

It was an experience which, I am sure, none of us who were present is ever likely to forget, for in imagination – and not wholly in imagination either – we had been present at the funeral ceremonies of a king long dead and almost forgotten. At a quarter past two we had filed down into the tomb, and when, three hours later, hot, dusty, and dishevelled, we came out once more into the light of day, the very valley seemed to have changed for us and taken on a more personal aspect. We had been given the Freedom.

The treasure of the Incas

Ever since the death of the Inca Atahualpa and the final conquest of Peru men have remained convinced that splendid golden treasures lie buried in the Peruvian mountains. The most important of these hoards is known as the Inca Treasure. It consists of the gold – an estimated £250,000,000 worth – which was on its way to Caxamalca as part of Atahualpa's ransom. It is said that when news of his death arrived the gold convoys turned back and their precious cargoes were buried. Ever since then, men and women have been obsessed by the rumour of this treasure and the fact that there is no clear evidence that it actually exists has never deterred the innumerable expeditions which have set out to find it.

All these expeditions have come from abroad or been conducted by foreigners. Why have the Indians themselves made no attempt to find the gold of their ancestors and reclaim their former glory? This question intrigued the German naturalist Alexander von Humboldt when he visited Caxamalca at the beginning of the nineteenth century. In his book, *Views of Nature*, published in 1849, he describes his visit to the scene of Atahualpa's imprisonment and murder:

An interesting and amiable youth of seventeen conducted us over the ruins of the ancient palace. Though living in the utmost poverty, his imagination was filled with images of the subterranean splendour and the golden treasures which, he assured us, lay hidden beneath the heaps of rubbish over which we were treading. He told us that one of his ancestors once blindfolded the eyes of his wife, and then, through many intricate passages cut in the rock, led her down into the subterranean gardens of the Inca. There the lady beheld, skilfully imitated in the purest gold, trees laden with leaves and fruit, with birds perched on their branches. Among other things, she saw Atahualpa's gold sedan-chair which had been so long searched for in vain, and which is alleged to have sunk in the basin at the Baths of Pultamarca. The husband commanded his wife not to touch any of these enchanted treasures, reminding her that the period fixed for the restoration of the Inca empire had not yet arrived, and that whosoever should touch any of the treasures would perish that same night. These golden dreams and fancies of the youth were founded on recollections and traditions transmitted from remote times. Golden gardens, such as those alluded to, have been described by various writers who allege that they actually saw them ... They are said to have existed beneath the Temple of the Sun at Cuzco, at Caxamalca, and in the lovely valley of Yucay, which was a favourite seat of the sovereign family ...

The son of Astorpilca assured me that under-

Hidden gold

ground, a little to the right of the spot on which I then stood, there was a large Datura tree, or Guanto, in full flower, exquisitely made of gold wire and plates of gold, and that its branches overspread the Inca's chair. The morbid faith with which the youth asserted his belief in this fabulous story, made a profound and melancholy impression on me. These illusions are cherished among the people here, as affording them consolation amidst great privation and earthly suffering. I said to the lad, 'Since you and your parents so firmly believe in the existence of these gardens, do you not, in your poverty, sometimes feel a wish to dig for the treasures that lie so near you?'

The young Peruvian's answer was so simple and so expressive of the quiet resignation peculiar to the aboriginal inhabitants of the country, that I noted it down in Spanish in my journal. 'Such a desire,' said he, 'never comes to us. My father says that it would be sinful. If we had the golden branches, with all their golden fruits, our white neighbours would hate us and injure us. We have a little field and good wheat. That is enough.' Few of my readers will, I trust, be displeased that I have recalled here the words of young Astorpilca and his golden dreams.

In 1967 two young Englishmen, Mark Howell and Tony Morrison, decided to try and find the legendary treasure. They studied the ancient Inca gold routes in an attempt to locate the areas where the gold could have been conveniently hidden when news came of the king's death. It was then that they learned of the existence of a deep cave, a cave that was rumoured to contain a lake. It seemed a likely place to hide – and find – a treasure. In their book *Steps to a Fortune*, Howell and Morrison described their exploration of the mysterious cave of Sorata:

Despite its small entrance the cavern soon opened to a gigantic size and we had only a few

In 1967 two young Englishmen tried to find the lost treasure of the Incas. They heard about the cave of Sorata with its deep mysterious lake and it was here that their search began. Here, one of them is seen setting off across the lake for the first time

yards to crawl on our bellies. Eighty yards inside a most enormous roof fall had occurred; perhaps ten thousand tons of boulders and rubble were piled there. Shining the torches upward, we could see the outline of the vast hole it had torn in the roof, but their beams could not plumb its centre.

From the top of this subterranean mountain was a view of a level sandy floor some way below. This stretched away out of sight. I do not suppose that the 'mountain' was more than fifty feet high, if that, but in that underground world, climbing down it was like acting out some fantasy of Jules Verne. In places the sand showed faint marks of a stream bed: though where water could have come from – with the cave mouth facing on to a one thousand foot slope down to a river – no one could suggest. A walk along the sand floor

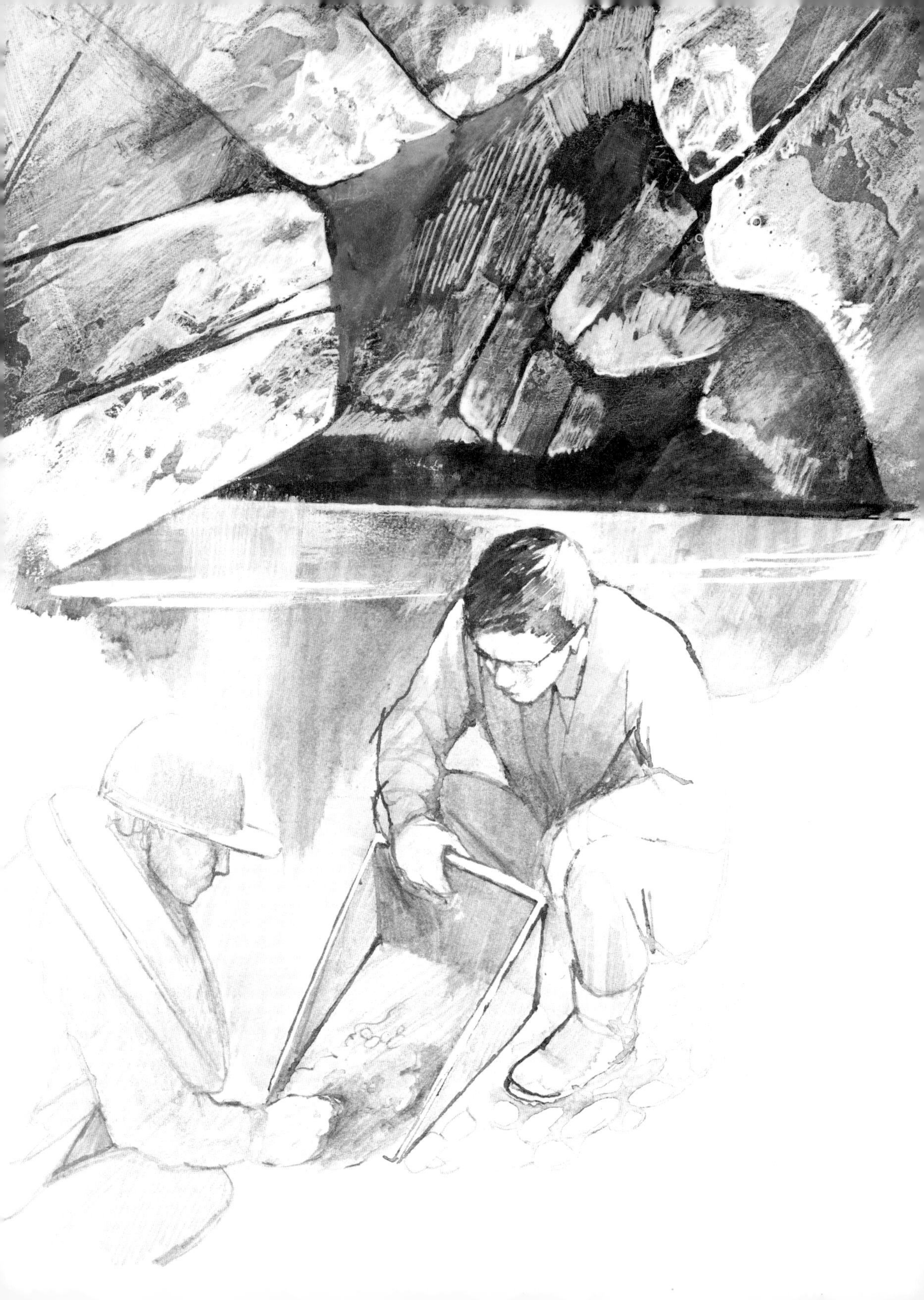

brought us eventually to a beach. Beyond, water spread away as far as the torch beams would reach, flat and motionless as a sheet of plate glass.

I connected our five hundred watt searchlight to the accumulator, pointed it over the lake and flipped on the switch. We gazed in startled and excited silence as the powerful beam lit up a chamber two hundred yards long, with a grey, gently arching roof fifty feet up. Along the sheer walls bordering the lake, thin spires of limestone, like broken razor blades, showed just above the surface. Though we could not have been the first people to enter the cave, I am sure that we were the first to see it in its entirety. Very far away across the lake the beam fell dimly on a wall facing us. The lake was roughly T-shaped, with the beach on which we were, at the bottom of the stem of the T. The distant wall we could see extended out of sight in both directions along invisible arms of the lake. In its independence of geological common sense, and in its majestic nature, the cavern seemed to hint that our suspicions of its past were well-founded ...

We had brought with us a metal drag, or square-shaped bucket, so attached to a line that it could be dragged underwater and scoop up material lying on the lake bed. It was an impromptu apparatus but in operation it was reasonably efficient. One man would take it out on to the lake in the boat and drop it into the water. Whichever way it landed, it would still present a scraping edge to the bottom. It was then hauled carefully in, with the sediment it scraped up.

We had expected to find mud on the bottom, but perhaps only a thin layer covering the bed rock. And in this we hoped to discover clues as to whether men had ever worked or lived in the cave. We realized that a few people must have wandered in from curiosity, but thought it unlikely that they would have gone beyond the beach of the lake. It would have been a brave man who swam out into the lake, without a strong light, with those sharp limestone spikes sticking up in places. Certainly, it was only the boat and the powerful light which made it possible for us to explore the lake in safety. We were therefore confident that whatever the drag brought up would be of natural origin, or material deposited by people who had carried out work here on a similar or greater scale than our own – namely the Incas. We did not expect to find beer bottles. We didn't.

The substance we brought up was a brittle sludge of some pale pink and white material. It was neither rock nor mud, but seemed more like a kind of decomposed rock. We wondered for a time whether a chemical in the water might have corroded the lake bed in some curious way. The only way to find out, it seemed, was to try and cut through this deposit to the rock beneath ...

There was no way of finding how thick the deposit was, though we knew that it was in one place two and a half feet thick at least. Tim calculated that dredging even that thickness from the whole of the lake would be an undertaking lasting years rather than weeks. And it might easily be two or three times thicker. Someone suggested pumping out the lake with a petrol powered pump, but someone else pointed out that this would exhaust the oxygen in the cave and very likely cause roof falls as well. A pump installed outside would face the farcical task of sucking water up a vertical distance of nearly seventy feet. And yet; there must be *some* way. Somewhere below that peaceful surface there might lie a king's ransom!

But the Inca's captain, if he had chosen this as a hiding place, had chosen with a perfection that almost suggested prescience. He, knowing where a hoard was, could have found it quite quickly; we had shown that several feet of sediment could be removed quite quickly and without elaborate apparatus. But unless a searcher knew where to look he would be faced with the hopeless task of removing thousands of tons of material in a search for something *that might not be there*. Even the metal detector was of no use because of the blanketing effect of the slightly

117

conductive lake water. If anything *did* lie there, it was safe. Had we known for certain that the treasure was there, we might have been prepared to devote years to the task of finding it. But it needs only an element of doubt to baulk at such a project. It is contemptible to withdraw if there is a sporting chance with some slight element of danger, or at the prospect of hard work for a while. But if a danger of obsession obtrudes, as clearly here it would have to – to devote enormous labour to an endeavour that might easily prove fruitless – it is madness to continue ... We had learned an important lesson in treasure-hunting; that of tactical withdrawal.

The Inca Treasure, if it exists, has yet to be found. It is unlikely, though, that men will ever stop searching for it.

The wreck of the Laurentic

No one knows whether golden treasure really does lie beneath the calm waters of the lake in the cave of Sorata. Other underwater treasures, though, have held less mystery. Submerged Spanish galleons in Caribbean and Californian waters have always attracted treasure seekers and, off our own coast, the cargoes of Spanish ships wrecked after the Armada have been investigated by gold hunters.

People who hunt for underwater gold are faced with particular problems. Deep-sea diving demands special skills from the treasure seeker, and elaborate equipment may be needed if a wreck is particularly deep or if it lies in stormy waters.

These skills were certainly needed when naval divers started to recover the golden cargo of the *Laurentic*. This ship was a White Star liner which set sail for the United States in January 1917 with a cargo of gold worth £5,000,000 as payment for war munitions. But the gold never got across the Atlantic. The *Laurentic* was torpedoed off the northern coast of Ireland and sank, taking the gold – and two hundred members of the crew – to the sea bed. It was obvious that the gold could not be allowed to remain in its watery hiding-place, and a diving team, led by Captain G. C. C. Damant, set about the task of recovering it. At first the job seemed easy: the *Laurentic* was lying a mere twenty fathoms down. But the hull of the ship was badly damaged and therefore dangerous, and to make matters worse, the Atlantic Ocean was stormy, treacherous and unpredictable. The task was so difficult that divers worked for seven years before all the gold was recovered.

In 1926, Captain Damant wrote an article about the *Laurentic* salvage operations for the *Journal of Hygiene*. In it, he described the difficulties which his divers had faced:

Let us follow the actions of one of the divers. He has been dressed and put into the water some minutes beforehand and is waiting just below the surface for the word to go down. Four minutes before it is time for his predecessor to leave the wreck the order is given and he slides rapidly down the thin wire 'shot-rope' which is put on afresh daily and leads directly to the spot where the work is being done. To slide down the 126 feet takes a minute or slightly less: the increase in atmospheric pressure of fifty-five pounds per square inch produces no physiological effect, though of course the descending diver has frequently to force open his Eustachian tubes. On first reaching the wreck he hauls down thirty feet or so of his own air pipe, ties it with a lanyard to some convenient part of the wreck and gives the order by telephone: 'Haul taut air pipe.' Those above pull it up into as nearly a straight line as the tide will allow, so that there is no curving bight of pipe flowing out and liable to catch in distant parts of the wreck. The lanyard of course prevents any of the strain from coming on to the diver, whom it would pull off the bottom. The diver can generally see twenty feet or so, beyond which distance all is vague mist. He has landed in the bottom of a sort of crater the sides of which are formed by jagged shelves of plate, each one piled high with toppling masses of broken wood and indescribable junk.

Near the bottom of the shot-rope stands a large hopper or bucket, painted white so as to be conspicuous in the general gloom, into which a diver is struggling to lift a bulging sack. It is to help him that our friend has gone down early: he stumbles across, gives a heave to the sack, and seeing it flop into the bucket with the raising of a cloud of black mud, turns his back and makes for a canvas hose close at hand. This hose terminates in a specially strong conical metal pipe about two feet long. The diver gets down flat on the sandy floor of the crater, grips the metal pipe in his right hand, and asks for the water to be turned on from above. With a powerful jet issuing, the nozzle can be thrust deep into the caked silt and the diver's left hand follows it up, exploring this way and that among the pebbles, chunks of iron and other hard objects buried in the sand. It is now absolutely pitch dark on account of the cloud of mud and dirt raised by the hose; and if a gold bar comes to hand the diver lays it behind in contact with his leg.

Twelve minutes after leaving the surface he gets the order to start bagging sand and the water is stopped. With one of the bags already described he gets to work on the loosened dirt, scraping it in with his bare hands or a bit of wood.

Perhaps during the hosing period he has located bars without being able to work them out, and he will now direct his digging towards them, bringing a knife or a crowbar to bear and working against time: for after thirteen minutes on the bag the order to 'Come up' is given from above. He has five minutes now in which to put his bars, if any, into the bucket, lift in his heavy sack of sand, and gather up into coils the slack pipe between himself and the lanyard. Giving the order, 'Up pipe', he casts off the lanyard, watches his pipe go up all clear, and then throttles the air-escape valve on his helmet so that in a moment he is sliding rapidly up the shot-rope again. Thirty feet below the surface (the exact spot being indicated to him from above) he checks his ascent, and letting go the wire shot-rope swings through the water to a short hanging rope steadied by a weight at the end.

There he passes through the decompression period. Adjusting his buoyancy so as to be only slightly negative, he can maintain his position on the rope with one hand or one leg while violently exercising his other three limbs and trunk with the object of increasing the circulation and consequently the rate of escape of nitrogen from his tissues. After spending five minutes thirty feet below the surface he is signalled to ascend another ten feet, and after spending ten more minutes in the same way at the new level he is called up to his final stage ten feet below the surface, where fifteen minutes are passed. On getting inboard some sixty-five or seventy minutes after entering the water he is undressed, in some cases breathes oxygen for some minutes, and then starts deck work, attending to the other divers' pipes and so on. This is hard physical work, but not comparable to the half-hour spent in the wreck.

The gold bars or ingots generally lay eighteen inches or two feet deep in the sand, so that the men could only reach them with their finger tips. As soon as the hose stopped playing, or one let go of it so as to bring both hands to bear on a bar, the sand would settle down and firmly grip the arms plunged into it. Some layers of deposit were too firm to be broken up by the hose with the highest water-pressure we could apply. As a rule we did not go above seventy pounds per square inch, as the loosened pebbles, etc., in flying about would batter and bruise the divers' hands. Apart from this type of damage the men's hands got into a pitiful state when a spell of fine weather enabled diving to be pushed on for six or eight days in succession. The finger-nails used to get worn down to a strip barely a quarter of an inch wide; and the outer layers of skin on the extremity of each finger would be rubbed away so as to leave a raw surface about half an inch across. The pain of this condition was specially bad at night after the day's work was over, and the less injured skin which had been soaked in salt water all day began to dry and shrink ...

Leathern gauntlets were available in unlimited quantities, but the men would not wear them as long as they could use their bare hands at all. The reason for this was that they used to distinguish ingots from other hard objects deep down in the sand by touch alone; and the gloves, though by no means stiff ones, baulked this sense. Of course the shape and weight of a gold bar were unmistakable to anyone who could *handle* it, but here the divers usually had to make their minds up by what they could feel of one small part of the surface of a deeply buried bar with the tips of their fingers. Experienced divers of the greatest keenness and skill coming to us did not compare favourably with our old hands till they had been working six months on the job; and I believe that what they chiefly lacked at first, and were acquiring in the interval, was this delicate finger-tip sense. They missed bars and used to spend time laboriously working out chunks of brass or glazed porcelain ware.

It will probably strike the reader that half an hour on the bottom is rather a short dive; and so it would be for most purposes. At the beginning, when divers good enough for the job were scarce, long dives formed the only possible means of getting anything done; and later on, for special purposes, we sometimes kept a man down in the wreck for a long period. But as we got together a team of experts who could start effective work within a minute of landing in the wreck, and needed no time for making themselves comfortable or thinking how to get over some difficulty, it turned out much better to get a perfectly fresh man to work every half-hour. It somehow quickened activity and mental alertness on deck as well as under water to have fresh news and viewpoints at such frequent intervals; and it nourished the invaluable spirit of competition.

'All the gold in Germany'

The *Laurentic* was a casualty of the First World War. But gold was also to be lost – and found – during the dark days of the Second World War. Just before war was declared, Adolf Hitler sent a gift of gold worth 6,000,000 marks to his friend and ally the Italian dictator Mussolini. The Lufthansa plane which was carrying the gold never reached Milan; it vanished somewhere over the Swiss Alps. Fragments of the aircraft were later found but the gold was never recovered, and the treasure still lies buried in the ice and snow of the Gemelli Glacier.

Golden treasures of a different kind were to be discovered as the war ended. Garry Hogg has told the story in his book *Lust for Gold*:

Early in April 1945 the 90th Infantry Division of the American Third Army overran a district to the south-west of Eisenach, where there is a substantial salt-mining industry. Military police engaged on checking civilian movement behind the lines stopped two German women hurrying along a minor road. They claimed that they were going in search of a midwife on behalf of a neighbour, and the military police accepted their

The gold reserves of the Third Reich. General Patton's Third Army found something like a hundred tons of gold bullion plus vast amounts of currency and art treasures in a salt-mine near Eisenach. This shows one of the tunnels in the mine stacked high with currency

story, which seemed genuine enough. As though in gratitude for the gesture, one of the women pointed across a field and said: 'There is a salt-mine over there. And in it is all the gold in Germany.'

The clue was followed up. The salt-mine proved to consist of some miles of underground passages and chambers of varying sizes, some of them open and manifestly empty, others with massive doors that were locked, barred and sealed. In one of them was found a collection of paintings by Rembrandt, Raphael, Van Dyck and Dürer, together with a chest containing a number of valuable manuscripts by Goethe. But, so far, no gold.

However, at the end of an apparently endless underground passage the searchers eventually came face to face with a door more massively armoured than any of the others. It resisted all attempts to open it, and finally a stick or two of gelignite had to be strategically placed and then exploded.

The door was blown neatly off its hinges. And what a sight met the eyes of the engineers as the smoke began to thin out! Canvas bags were stacked on the floor by the hundred; and each bag, when it had been opened, proved to contain ingots of gold weighing forty pounds apiece. There were larger sacks filled to bursting with British gold sovereigns and Italian gold twenty-lire pieces; there were vast numbers of smaller canvas bags each containing a number of much smaller gold bars than the forty-pound ingots – but pure gold all the same – some six inches long by three inches in width and almost an inch thick; there were fifty large sacks containing gold coin in the currency of many countries: Turkish pounds, Norwegian gold crowns, American, Spanish, Portuguese and other gold coins of many denominations. In all, there were many millions of pounds' worth. If there was not, as the grateful woman had said, 'all the gold in Germany', there was nevertheless a pretty substantial portion of it; and one well worth the finding!

Nor was it the only big haul made at the end of World War II. Only two months later some men of the American Third Division, their noses scenting gold, penetrated into the private cellars of the Burgomaster of Bad Gastein. Buried beneath the paved floor they found a number of massive metal-lined wooden chests and a greater number of heavy canvas bags. All of these were wired and stamped with the seal of the German Legation in Berne, Switzerland. They proved to contain a great quantity of British, American and Italian gold bar and coin – to a value of more than £7,000,000. Careful investigation revealed that this treasure had for some time been concealed on Ribbentrop's estate beside Lake Fuschl, not very far from Salzburg and within view of Hitler's famous Eagle's Eyrie high above Berchtesgaden. It had been moved on his personal instructions when the advance of the Allies became too threatening.

Two men of the US Army Finance Corps checking the bags of currency

Inside one of the strong-rooms with the gold bars stacked on the floor and in the racks

Lasseter's reef

The prospect of finding hidden gold, be it in the shape of Spanish doubloons or German ingots, has always been enticing. But golden treasure can take other forms, and men have risked their lives trying to find legendary reefs of gold and long-lost mines of enormous richness. Harold Bell Lasseter was such a man.

In 1929, Lasseter announced that he had discovered a rich reef of gold, six miles (9·7 kilometres) long, in the desert of central Australia. His story convinced many eminent authorities, and an expedition set out with Lasseter as a guide. But the party quarrelled, and Lasseter travelled on alone, accompanied only by a few camels. He was never seen again.

A search party later found diaries and letters which Lasseter had written on his last journey. The extracts from these which follow are taken from Ion L. Idriess's book *Lasseter's Last Ride*.

Blacks tried to kill me today while I was waiting ... three spears were thrown but two shots drove them off one spear landed in the tree I had my back against within three inches of my neck the other two were on the side – they have smoked in the whole tribe I saw three big smokes – a lot of blacks moving for the camp... will make fo ... and thence to the ... and may reach ... These blacks seem ... and gave me a rabbit they he ... so I gave them my remaining blanket ... one old fellow took a fancy to my hat, which was falling to pieces, so I gave it ... him ... have tied my head ... a ... point out the camel pad to th ... young men and told them they could have all they could ...

They seemed to unders ... a good deal and I tried ... them to send a message by ... smoke signals to Alice Spgs.

Rene Darling,

Don't grieve for me. I've done my best and have pegged the reef, not strictly according to law as the blacks pinched my miners right and I don't know the number but I photographed the datum post on the Quartz Blow the post is sticking in the water hole and the photo faces north.

I made the run in 5 days but the blacks have a sacred place nearby and will pull the peg up for sure.

I've taken the films and will plant them at Winter's Glen if I can get there the Blight has got me beat.

Take good care of Bobby, Betty, and Joy please, I want Bobby to be a Civil Engineer try and educate him for that.

Darling I do love you so I'm sorry I can't be with you at the last but God's will be done.

Yours ever,
x Harry xxx

Later in the day the black who had first raided my camp showed up and told the tribe that I had tried to shoot him.

I had only turned in about an hour when 20 of them came down, woke me up and told me they were going to kill me, the headman who is so treacherous being the leader and spokesman. I succeeded in bluffing them by talking a lot and refusing to get up. I told them ... and they postponed the killing till tomorrow ... (he heard me yell 'I'll shoot') ... as soon as I was assured they had retired I rose and made a moonlight flit for five miles back to the cave again (the old fellow had moved my camp for me to where rabbits were more plentiful) now that tomorrow is here and they find I have moved I expect an attack in force tonight. In the dust of the cave I have just unearthed an unexpected find 5 revolver cartridges tho' as they know I am practically blind that may not avail me much. Two or more spears were carried by each man. No doubt they were in deadly earnest too. So I don't suppose I've an earthly chance of surviving. I can carry 2 gallons and 3 pints of water but that is hardly likely to take me the 80 miles to Mt. Olga and on no food whatever. I've brought this all on myself by going alone but I thought the blacks, tho' primitive, were fair dealing. Good Bye and God Bless you Rene darling wife of mine and may God Bless the children.

Harry.

... it is now 25 days since the camels bolted – allowing 10 days to Ilbilba they should be near home by now, then people will speculate a week as to where I am then someone will be sent to Ilbilba a black probably who will loiter on the way – then too late camels will be ... despatched over my route 360 miles via Ilbilba and a motor truck could get to me in two days if they ...

I have taken up 10 holes in my waist belt and still it is loose so you can see how I have fallen away. I'm just a skeleton now and I always thou ... of the black till now, only 2 weeks ago or less I made them some beautiful ... now they are waiting for me to die in order to steal my shirt and trousers off the body ...

Darling I want you to remember me as when we first met and not the scarecrow that I now am. Have shrunk still further and the flies and ants have nearly eaten my face away. I can do nothing against them 'beaten by Sandy Blight' what an epitaph ...

I've tried to amuse the blacks by drawing pictures but somehow they don't appeal. I am as helpless as a kitten now and they know it. I was turned adrift this morning and told to shift for myself ...

I have watched and hoped for relief till I am about the end of my tether ... with lots of water I can hold out for several days yet but agony of starvation may drive me to shoot myself.

I think it the worst possible death with one experience of this country I should never have gone alone but I relied on Paul to follow me what good a reef worth millions I would give it all for a loaf of bread and to think that only a week away is lots of tucker the blacks are not troubling me now they know I'm dying and will wait ...

Good Bye Rene darling wife mine and don't grieve remember you must live for the children now dear, but it does seem cruel to die alone out here because I have always been good to blacks.

– my last prayer is 'God be merciful to me as a sinner and be good to those I leave behind.'

xxx Harry x

The search for the fabulous reef did not end with Lasseter's death. In 1936 another expedition set out to find it, led by a senior government geologist. This expedition failed to discover the reef but, as it turned out, this was hardly surprising. The expedition found that the country where Lasseter had supposedly located the reef was composed of sandstone and never could and never would contain gold or any other metal.

The curse of the Lost Dutchman

Harold Bell Lasseter was not the first man to die in search of gold which didn't exist, and he won't be the last. His story is a tragic one, but the story of the Lost Dutchman Mine is far more mysterious and sinister.

The Superstition Mountains lie about forty miles to the east of Phoenix, Arizona. A rich gold mine was discovered there by a man named Jacob Waltz, who died in 1891 taking the secret of its location with him. Ever since then men and woman have travelled to the Superstitions to search for the legendary Lost Dutchman Mine. Many of them have never returned and many of them have died in suspicious circumstances. The story of the mine and of the men who have looked for it has been told by Curt Gentry is his book *The Killer Mountains*. The title is not as theatrical as it may seem for, as the following extracts show, the Superstition Mountains have not dealt kindly with those who have tried to uncover their golden secret:

Elisha M. Reavis was often called 'The Madman of the Superstitions'. From 1872 to the time of his death in 1896, Reavis resided in a remote part of the Superstition range, raising giant vegetables (a head of Reavis cabbage often weighed ten pounds) and no small amount of local speculation as to why he was never bothered by the Apaches. The secret apparently was that the Apaches thought him mad – it was said he ran naked in the canyons at night, shooting his pistol at the stars – and the Indians held madmen in superstitious awe. Someone – or something – caught up with him, however, for in April 1896, when a friend realized Reavis was overdue his periodic trip into town, a search was made and his badly decomposed body found next to his campfire. He had apparently been eaten by coyotes, though, from the habits of these creatures, it was surmised this had occurred some time after his death. His severed head was found some distance away.

Reavis' was the first recorded beheading ...

In 1927 a Jersey City, New Jersey, man and his two sons were hiking in the Superstitions when someone began rolling rocks down on them from the cliffs above, crushing the leg of one of the boys. The following year two deer hunters were driven out of the mountains by huge rocks rolling down on them ...

In 1932 two Phoenix hikers – Calvin Blaine and Ray Schweiger – were shot at by a long-range rifle. Only by hiding behind rocks and waiting until nightfall were they able to leave the area safely ...

In 1937 an old prospector, Guy 'Hematite' Frink, came out of the Superstitions with some rich gold samples and a report of being shot at. In November 1938, Frink was found shot in the stomach alongside a trail in the mountains. A small sack of gold ore was beside him. His death was listed as 'accidental'.

In June of 1947 ... sixty-two-year-old James A. Cravey, a retired photographer, made a much publicized trip into the Superstitions by helicopter in search of the Lost Dutchman Mine. The pilot set him down in La Barge Canyon, within sight of Weaver's Needle. When Cravey failed to hike out as planned, a search was launched, but though his camp was found, Cravey wasn't. The following February his headless skeleton was found in a canyon in the vicinity of Bluff Springs Mountain, a good distance from his camp. It was tied in a blanket and lay on a trail that had been searched previously. His skull was found later, in a hackberry thicket twenty-five to thirty feet from the rest of his skeleton. Despite these extraordinary circumstances, the coroner's jury ruled, 'No evidence of foul play.'

In February 1951, Dr John Burns, a physician from Oregon, parked his car about a mile from Goldfield and hiked into the Superstitions. He was found that night, shot through the guts, less than three-quarters of a mile from his car ... Although a ballistics expert testified that the absence of powder burns and the angle of the wound ruled out the possibility that the injury was self-inflicted, the coroner's jury brought in a verdict of accidental death.

Joseph H. Kelley, of Dayton, Ohio, commenced his search for the Lost Dutchman early in the spring of 1952. He was never seen again. In May 1954, a skeleton was found in a canyon in the vicinity of Weaver's Needle which may have been Kelley's. The man had been shot directly from above. His death was listed as accidental shooting.

Two California boys, Charles G. Harshberger and Ross A. Bley, hiked into the Superstitions the same year as Kelley and nothing further was heard of them. It may be that they slipped out unseen. It is also possible that they had not told their parents of their destination, and their families never knew to contact the Arizona authorities. Three Texas youths, whose names were never known, had vanished similarly a few years earlier.

In February 1955, four Tucson youths went into the Superstitions on a javelina hunt, armed with .22s. One, Charles Massey, sighted a pig and chased it, leaving the others behind. His body was found the following day, five miles from where he was last seen, wedged between two boulders at the base of a cliff from which he had fallen or been shoved after being shot between the eyes with a heavy-calibre rifle. The coroner's verdict – 'Accidental shooting from ricochet bullet.' To repeat, Massey's own rifle was a .22 ...

In January 1956, a Brooklyn man reported to police that his brother, Martin Zywotho, had been missing for several weeks and that he was afraid he had gone into the Superstition Mountains in Arizona in search of the Lost Dutchman Mine. In February some javelina hunters found a badly decomposed body near a deserted campsite. There was a bullet hole just above the right temple and a .38 calibre six-shooter with three empty chambers. The body was subsequently identified as Zywotho's, and after tracing the serial numbers on the gun, it was proven that it had been purchased by him. The verdict – 'Accidental shooting or possible suicide.' Oddly enough, however, the gun was found *under* Zywotho's body.

In April 1958, a deserted campsite was found a short distance in from the northern entrance of the mountains. There was a bloodstained blanket and handkerchief, a Geiger counter, cooking utensils, a gun cleaning kit but no gun, and some letters from which the names of the addressees had been torn. No trace of the camp's occupant was ever found.

One Saturday night that December, Roderick White, twenty-six, and his brother Ronald, twenty-two, met a pretty waitress at the Black Swan Restaurant in Phoenix. She was Nettie Isore Maxey, seventeen. When the young men said they were going hiking in the Superstitions the following day, she asked to go along. Once in the mountains the group became separated.

After calling her name for several hours they found her, bloody but still breathing, at the base of an eighty-foot cliff from which she had apparently fallen. She was pronounced dead on arrival at Mesa Hospital at 8 p.m. ...

On 23 October 1960 a group of hikers found a headless skeleton near the foot of a cliff. The skull, discovered four days later, was pierced by two large-calibre bullets. The body was subsequently identified as that of Franz Harrer, an Austrian exchange student. Although the FBI (called in in this instance because Harrer was an alien) stated that they had a prime suspect, no arrest was ever made. Coroner's verdict – 'Death at the hands of person or persons unknown' ...

In January 1961, a family was picnicking in the Superstitions when one of the children noticed a curious thing: the sand at his feet resembled a human face. Playfully, he kicked the sand away, uncovering a skeleton. It was subsequently identified as that of Hilmer Charles Bohen, a forty-seven-year-old Salt Lake City prospector. Bohen had been shot through the back. Coroner's verdict – 'Shot to death by person or persons unknown' ...

That June, Davis Calvert, twenty-five, of Phoenix, was hiking in the Superstitions when an 'unknown person' shot him in the arm.

That August, a sheriff's posse began searching for Jay Clapp, a prospector who had been working in the Superstitions off and on for about fifteen years. Clapp had last been seen on 1 July. The search was finally abandoned.

On 26 March 1963 Vance Bacon, a thirty-year-old mining engineer from Phoenix, fell 4500 feet from the top of Weaver's Needle. Bacon and his companion, Ray Gatewood, twenty, of Tempe, had been hired a few days earlier by Celeste Jones to open a mine on the side of the Needle. Mrs Jones was convinced there was gold in the plug. Bacon was descending on a rope to the spot when he suddenly screamed and fell straight down the east face of the Needle. When his body was finally recovered it was found that his gloves had been burned from his hands by the rope.

Gatewood was left stranded on top of the Needle. While rescue workers – including sheriff's deputies – were trying to reach him by helicopter, two bullets splattered on the rocks near them.

In February 1964, an elderly New York City couple was found murdered in an automobile parked at the edge of the Superstitions.

In March the camp and headless skeleton of Jay Clapp was finally located, three years after Clapp's disappearance. He was identified by two cameras with the initials 'JC' engraved on them. His skull has never been found and the cause of death remains 'unknown'.

In April two California men searching for the Dutchman quarrelled and one shot the other, although not fatally.

In February 1965, an old campsite was found in the north-west part of the Superstitions, about one mile south and a half-mile east of First Water. There was a set of false teeth, various human bone fragments, and a pillbox with the name Charles Reed, Wenatchee, Washington, and the date 10-3-63. Nothing more was found.

Some of these deaths can be explained, perhaps, but many cannot. Who was responsible? No one knows. Perhaps Jacob Waltz, the Dutchman, laid a curse on whoever came to find his mine. Or perhaps the brooding Superstition Mountains hold an even darker secret.

8. The hunt goes on

Two miles down

Legends of lost mines and buried treasure still lure men to risk their lives to find gold. But the day of the individual prospector has gone. Gold mining today is a complex enterprise, and elaborate machinery has replaced the pick and pan. Modern transport and methods of communication have reduced the dangers and difficulties of prospecting, and there is little excitement or adventure to be found on a present-day goldfield.

The largest gold-mining area in the world is on the Witwatersrand in South Africa where 78 per cent of the free world's gold is mined around Johannesburg. The largest gold mine there covers 12,100 acres (4900 hectares), and its main tunnels, if placed end to end, would stretch for 2600 miles (4200 kilometres). The richest mine in the area, Crown Mines, has produced 49·4 million ounces (1·4 million kilograms) of gold since it was opened.

Rich new goldfields have been discovered

Above: *the Western Deep Levels Mine – one of the famous deep gold mines of South Africa. Note the enormous mine dumps in the background*

A fortune in gold bullion

further south, in the Orange Free State, and it is there, at Carletonville, that the world's deepest mine is to be found. The Western Deep Levels Mine reached a depth of over two miles in 1975. The rock temperature at the lowest level often reaches 126°F (52·2°C) and refrigerated ventilation is needed to make work possible.

The modern goldfield is a far cry from the creeks and gullies of California and the Klondike. But the wealth and prosperity of the South African gold industry have been firmly based on the hardship and labour of the Africans who dig the gold, miles beneath the ground. Ernest Cole, a black South African photographer, has described the life and conditions of the miners in his moving book *House of Bondage*:

The work of mining the gold – and three tons of earth from shafts two miles deep must be sifted to yield one ounce – falls entirely to Africans. Twenty-four hours a day, six days a week, half a million Africans are at work in the earth. Of course, the mining companies also employ many whites, but all in supervisory capacities. Even those working underground, and designated as miners, never touch pick or shovel or drilling machines. The brute work is done by Africans, although they are never given the dignity of being called miner, only 'boy' – or 'boss boy' if they head up a work gang, the highest job to which they can aspire.

Labour for the mines works under contract and is recruited in the back-country tribal areas by mining company agents. Some men come from Lesotho and Botswana, others from as far away as Zambia and Angola. It is one of the rigidities of South African administration that the mines are permitted to import labour in droves, but that an outlander who crosses the border looking for work is subject to arrest and deportation... The African can be discharged, but he cannot quit. If he tries to escape he is branded a deserter and mine detectives from a special squad are sent to track him down...

The living conditions of the men who work the mines of South Africa are miserable almost beyond imagining – worse even than in the worst slums of Johannesburg. The miners are quartered in long, brick-walled structures with corrugated iron roofs. They live twenty to a room that measures eighteen by twenty-five feet. Each man has a concrete cubicle, the slab floor of which is his bed. What little furniture the common room contains – a few rough wooden tables and benches – is made by the occupants. Threadbare tunics and trousers hang about; it is a jungle of clothes. The most privacy a man can get is to hang a blanket in front of his bunk.

Plumbing is not only ancient but inadequate. Shower rooms are crowded with men trying to bathe while others do their meagre laundry.

Food? Ask a man what the food is like and he says, 'Like pig's food.' At mealtimes the men line up to have their ration ladled out by a kitchen employee who uses a shovel to slop the porridge onto their plates. Each man must show a job ticket; only those who have worked may eat.

Breakfast is at 5 a.m. and consists of sour porridge and coffee. Lunch, after the first shift ends between 1 and 3 p.m., is *nyula*, a stew of cabbage, carrots, and other vegetables, and sometimes meat, plus maize porridge. Supper is maize porridge and beans. The men crowd into their stuffy rooms to eat or squat outdoors. There is no dining hall, although there is a bar serving beer and hard liquor. Whenever possible the men go outside the compound to buy extra food – corn meal, for instance – which they cook themselves.

Sunday is the mine worker's day off, but boredom makes this almost the worst day of all. Separated from their families, with recreation facilities almost non-existent, the men mostly sit outside their rooms, doing nothing. Some sleep. Others take a walk or sew new patches on their ragged clothing.

To relieve the tedium, a number of men participate in programmes of tribal dances – the so-called 'mine dances' – which are a big tourist attraction for whites visiting Johannesburg. The dances are said to be entertainment for the

Working in a gold mine
Drilling
Queueing for food at lunchtime in the native 'cafeteria'

Gold and Gold-Hunters

blacks, but the audience in the stands is strictly segregated, and somehow the dancers always end up facing the whites and showing their backs to Africans. No admission is charged, but this is no more than fair considering that the performers do not get paid and that the audience is told, by signs on the walls, not even to toss a few coins into the arena as a tip...

At the end of his contract, the worker can sign on again, this time (and each subsequent term) for six months, or he may go home again.

If he chooses to leave, he... receives in a lump sum the money the mine management has been withholding for him. It is never very much, but it is a rare man who has set aside anything from his cash in hand, and it gives him a chance to reach home with something in his pocket. If he quits at the end of his first contract, he is given a bonus certificate which entitles him to a two-cent-a-day rise should he decide within six months to sign on again. If he waits longer than six months, or loses his certificate, he starts over again at the beginning rate...

The majority of miners re-enlist when their contracts are up. Poor as a mine living is, for those men it is even poorer at home. One will tell you, 'I'll be going home when the drought ends.' But it never does, and life in the mines goes on.

Finally, there are the men who never reach their contract's end. These are the unlucky victims of mine accidents or of phthisis, a deadly and so far incurable disease of the lungs, which is prevalent among South African miners. In either case, the man is returned... for hospitalization, cancellation of his contract, and discharge. The mine company arranges for him to get compensation, sometimes in instalments, which presumably protects the improvident African from spending all his money at one time or in one place. But it also means that outstanding balances need not be paid over a man's death and that, even in incapacity, a man does not have freedom to go his own way...

However they leave – sick, injured, worn out, or hale and hearty with the savings of twenty years' work... – they are never missed. For as they go out the gate, there are always new men coming in.

Nearly two thousand years separate Ernest Cole from Diodorus of Sicily, but their descriptions of the lives of miners in ancient Egypt and present-day South Africa have much – too much – in common.

Gold on your doorstep

Gold has been mined in Britain too. The Romans found it near Llandeilo in Dyfed and you can still visit their old workings at Dolaucothi. Further north, the old gold mines near Dolgellau have produced gold to the value of £9,000,000 since the 1850s. In the 1860s there were gold rushes in that area and on the eastern coast of Scotland; they could not be compared with those in California or Australia but men did flock to Dolgellau and to Helmsdale to find gold. For a while.

People still hunt for gold in the streams of Wales and Scotland, and each year about thirty applications are made for permission to search for gold in Wales alone. But, before you set off with pan and pick, remember that permission must be obtained from the Crown Mineral Agents. This permission – if you can get it – does not give you automatic access to private property and, if you do find gold, the Government will demand a share of it, but, if you're lucky, you may well find traces of 'some kind of mettle that looks like goald' glinting in the bottom of your pan.

Gold mining in Britain

Above: *panning for gold in Wales*

Right: *officials and workmen at the entrance to the Clogau Mine, c. 1900*

Below: *Machinery at the Morgan gold mine, c. 1890*

Index

Alaska, 72
Alchemy, 23–9
Atahualpa, 37–44, 114
Australia, 44, 67–72, 92–9, 123–5
Australia and Its Gold Fields (Hargraves), 67
Aztecs, 35–6

Black Bart, 89–92
Brannan, Sam, 47
Bruff, J. Goldsborough, 50–51, 54; quoted, 50–54
Buffum, E. Gould, quoted, 87–9
Bushrangers, 92–9

California, 44, 45–59, 66, 86, 87–92
Canada, 72–86
Carmack, G. W., 72
Carter, Howard, 109–12; quoted, 109–14
Century's Sensations, A (Sapte), 99
Clacy, Ellen, 92; quoted, 92–6
Cole, Ernest, 130; quoted, 130–32
Columbus, Christopher, 31; quoted, 31–5
Cortés, Hernando, 35–6
Craig, William, quoted, 66
Croesus, 17–18

Damant, Captain G. C. C., 119; quoted, 119–21
Diodorus of Sicily, 20, 132; quoted, 20–22

Egypt, 20–22, 109–14
Eisenach, 121–3
El Dorado, 44

Ferdinand, King of Spain, 31, 35
Fort Knox, 108–9
Forty-niners, 47–59, 64

Gentry, Curt, quoted, 126–8
Getting Gold (Johnson), 69

'Gilded man', 44
Golden Colony, The (Wathen), 98
Goldfinger (Fleming), 109
Gold rushes
  California, 45–59
  Nevada, 59
  Australia, 67–72
  Alaska, 72
  Klondike, 72–86
  Scotland, 132
  Wales, 132
Great Stone of the Philosophers (Valentinus), 24
Green, Timothy, quoted, 106–7

Hard Road to Klondike, The (MacGowan), 82
Hargraves, Edward Hammond, 67, 72; quoted, 67–8, 72
Helvetius, 27; quoted, 27–9
Herodotus, 18, 19; quoted, 18, 19–20
History of the Conquest of Peru (Prescott), 37
Hogg, Garry, quoted, 90–92, 121–3
House of Bondage (Cole), 130
Howell, Mark, 115; quoted, 115–18
Humboldt, Alexander von, 44; quoted, 114–15

Incas, 37–44, 114–18
Isabella, Queen of Spain, 31

Johnson, J. C. F., quoted, 69

Killer Mountains, The (Gentry), 126
Klondike, 44, 72–86
Klondyke: Truth and Facts of the New El Dorado (Sola), 72

Lady's Visit to the Gold Diggings of Australia, A (Clacy), 92
Lake Guatavita, 44

Lasseter, Harold Bell, 124, 125; quoted, 124–5
Lasseter's Last Ride (Idriess), 124
Laurentic, 118–21
London, Jack, 78; quoted, 79
Lost Dutchman mine, 126–8
Lust for Gold (Hogg), 90, 121
Lydia, 17–18

MacDonald, Alexander, 79; quoted, 79–82
MacGowan, Michael, 82, 86; quoted, 82–6
Marshall, James, 45, 47; quoted, 45–7
Metamorphoses, The (Ovid), 17
Mexico, 35–6
Midas, 16–17
Mining
   Egypt, 20–22
   California, 45–7
   Australia, 67–72
   Alaska, 72
   Canada, 72–86
   South Africa, 129–32
   Wales, 132–3
   Scotland, 132
Montez, Lola, 66
Montezuma, 35–6
Morrison, Tony, 115; quoted, 115–18
My Adventures on the Australian Goldfields (Craig), 66

Nuggets, 11, 65

Ovid, quoted, 17

Peru, 36–44, 114–18

Philosopher's Stone, 23–9
Pindar, 16
Pizarro, Francisco, 37–44
Prescott, William H., 37; quoted, 37–44
Prospecting, 49, 54–63, 65, 67–9, 72–8

Robbery, 87, 89–102
Roughing It (Twain), 59

Sapte, W., quoted, 99–102
Scotland, 132
Sheba, Queen of, 19
Six Months in the Gold Mines (Buffum), 87
Smugglers, The (Green), 102
Smuggling, 102–7
Sola, A. E. Ironmonger, quoted, 72–8
Solomon, 18–19
Sorata cave, 115–18
South Africa, 44, 129–32
Superstition Mountains, 126–8
Sutter, John A., 45–6

Tomb of Tutankhamen, The (Carter), 109
Tutankhamen, 109–14
Twain, Mark, 59; quoted, 59–63

Valentinus, Basil, 24; quoted, 24–6
Views of Nature (Humboldt), 114

Wales, 132–3
Wathen, George, quoted, 98–9
Woods, Daniel, 55; quoted, 55–9